JOURNAL OF LAW AND CYBER WARFARE

Volume 6 | Winter 2018 | Issue 2

Resilience, Perseverance and Fortitude: Lessons from My Parents
Rhea Siers[*]

After my mother's recent death, I shared my eulogy for her with JLCW's Editor-In-Chief, Daniel Garrie. My parents were both Holocaust survivors who came to the United States for a better life. Their stories of survival still amaze me to this day and they truly represent the triumph of the human spirit. Daniel and I discussed their stories and how, in this technological world, resilience, perseverance and fortitude are still essential to ensure the continuity of progress.

In my classroom, I have occasionally found that a basic knowledge of history has been lost in our educational system and that even in the most technical arena, there is value in understanding the lessons from our past.

So, I will tell you my parents' stories very briefly. My father was the sole survivor of his family of seven. At the age of 15, he ran away from a small town in Poland after the Nazis occupied his town. Using his own street smarts, he traversed almost all of Eastern Europe and finally ended up as a partisan heroically fighting the Nazis. He managed to talk his way out of Eastern Europe after the war was over, ending up in Brussels, where he met my mother. My mother and her cousins were sent out of Belgium to find refuge just

[*] *Rhea Siers, J.D.* is currently the Senior Fellow for Cyber Policy and Law at the Institute for Information Infrastructure Protection and a member of the adjunct faculty at the Elliott School of International Affairs, GWU as well as Johns Hopkins University. She is also a Senior Subject Matter Expert at RANE, the Risk Analysis Network and Exchange and Special Counsel at Zeichner, Ellman and Krause in New York.

one week ahead of the Nazi occupation. They were arrested in France by the Vichy French authorities (collaborators with the Nazis), placed in a detention camp, and ultimately sent on a train to the Auschwitz concentration camp. But the train broke down and in those few extra days, her uncle managed to bribe Vichy officials to release them. Then they began an arduous journey across the Pyrenee Mountains to Spain, where they were jailed. They were ultimately released and lived in Madrid until the war was over.

My parents' families were decimated by the Holocaust, but they were not ready to give up. They started anew in the United States and raised their family with few relatives, but they replanted what had been uprooted by the evil of the Holocaust. Their lives were not easy and their memories were difficult, but they decided as they said, "to not give Hitler any more victories."

Why is this relevant to us in this cyber age? Simply because resilience is much more than a marketing catchword – it is our ability to aspire to the future and make things better for our families and all humankind. It reminds us that we need to ask the right questions about the use of technological or cyber power. It also reminds us that the tremendous power of technology must be harnessed for good; technology cannot be used to undermine democracy or support evil. And we need to persevere, to create the norms, to establish the guideposts that will allow us to use this power without fear while allowing creativity to flourish.

The challenges we face today in cyber warfare are quite different than those of the last century. But the core lessons I learned from my parents – resilience, perseverance and fortitude – are just as valuable today as in the dark days of WWII.

Responding to the Call for a Digital Geneva Convention: An Open Letter to Brad Smith and the Technology Community

Colonel David Wallace &
Lt. Colonel Mark Visger*

"They came together in 1949 in Geneva Switzerland and that is what led to the recognition that they needed the fourth Geneva Convention to protect civilians in times of war. Now it the time for us to call on governments to protect civilians on the internet in times of peace."

Brad Smith, President of Microsoft Incorporated

* *Colonel David Wallace* is Professor and Head of the Department of Law at the U.S. Military Academy, West Point, New York. *Lieutenant Colonel Mark Visger* is a Judge Advocate in the U.S. Army and an Assistant Professor in the Department of Law at the U.S. Military Academy. Colonel Wallace served as a Visiting Scholar at the NATO Cooperative Cyber Defence Centre of Excellence (CCD COE) in Tallinn, Estonia in 2017. Colonel Wallace would like to thank the NATO CCD COE Director, Merle Maigre, the Law Branch Chief, Lauri Aasmann, and all of the members of the Law Branch for their collegial assistance and support during the fellowship. The authors would like to thank Lieutenant Colonel Shane Reeves and Professor Robert Barnsby for their support and assistance. The views expressed herein are personal views and do not necessarily reflect those of the Department of Defense, the United States Army, the United States Military Academy, any other department or agency of the United States Government or the NATO CCD COE. The analysis presented herein stems from academic research of publicly available sources, not protected operational information.

ABSTRACT

In February 2017, Brad Smith, President of Microsoft, electrified the technology community with a speech to the RSA Conference calling for a "Digital Geneva Convention" to stem the flow of State cyber operations that have become endemic. Despite good intentions, Smith's call for a Digital Geneva Convention is based, in part, on a misunderstanding of the state of international law as it applies to cyber. In fact, there already exists a robustly developed set of international law norms, although enforcement of these norms remains problematic. In addition, Smith's call for a Digital Geneva Convention overlooks the need for States to agree to adopt such a treaty. Despite these limitations, tech sector involvement in the international law process has the potential to develop the law in a positive direction and should be encouraged. However, such tech sector involvement requires an appreciation for international law and the current state of the law as it applies to cyber operations. With this foundation, the tech sector will be able to properly engage in the international law process to develop the law applicable to cyber operations to address their concerns.

INTRODUCTION & BACKGROUND

At the RSA Conference in San Francisco on February 14, 2017, Brad Smith, the President of Microsoft Corporation, gave a keynote address entitled "Protecting and Defending against Cyberthreats in Uncertain Times."[1] Smith

---

[1] Brad Smith, Protecting and Defending against Cyberthreats in Uncertain Times, RSA Conference, https://www.rsaconference.com/videos/protecting-and-defending-

highlighted, among other things, the troubling fact that in recent years there has been an expansion of incidents of States engaging in cyber operations against other States.[2] Smith contended that the 2014 Sony cyber-attack by North Korea was a turning point.[3] In that operation, a group calling themselves "Guardians of Peace" hacked into Sony Pictures. The United States has alleged that the Guardians of Peace were a cyber proxy for North Korea.[4] The hackers stole confidential documents and data from the Hollywood studio and posted them online and deleted other files.[5] It is believed by U.S. government officials that North Korea used the Guardians of Peace to target Sony because it backed the film, "The Interview," which depicts an assassination plot against the North Korean leader, Kim Jong-Un.[6] Commenting on the incident, Smith noted that the Sony cyberattack was "not for espionage, not related to the military, but to attack a private company for engaging in freedom of expression around, as it turned out, not a terribly popular movie."[7]

Using militaristic language and imagery, Smith

---

against-cyberthreats-in-uncertain-times (last visited Jan. 16, 2018).

[2] *Id.*

[3] *Id.*

[4] Ellen Nakashima, Craig Timberg & Andrea Peterson, *Sony Pictures hack appears to be linked to North Korea, investigators say*, Washington Post (Dec. 3, 2014), https://www.washingtonpost.com/world/national-security/hack-at-sony-pictures-appears-linked-to-north-korea/2014/12/03/6c3c7e3e-7b25-11e4-b821-503cc7efed9e_story.html?utm_term=.8d3e4029c075. Smith showed this webpage on his slides while discussing this attack.

[5] *Id.*

[6] Andrea Peterson, *The Sony Pictures hack, explained*, Washington Post (Dec. 18, 2014), https://www.washingtonpost.com/news/the-switch/wp/2014/12/18/the-sony-pictures-hack-explained/?utm_term=.b8aac1f6ebdc (last visited Aug. 7, 2017).

[7] Smith, *supra* note 1.

described cyberspace as a new battlefield, albeit different than other war fighting domains of land, sea and air. Underscoring cyberspace's unique and different nature, Smith commented that cyberspace is owned and operated by the private sector whether "it's submarine cables or datacenters or servers or laptops or smartphones."[8] He also posited that companies like Microsoft are the "world's first responders" to cyberattacks by States.[9] After framing the problem of increased State cyber-attacks, Smith offered, for consideration, three responses to such actions. First, he argued for greater vigilance in that companies and individuals need to do more (and more together) in terms of cyber security even though there are many new and important things already being done.[10] Second, Smith laid out arguments for a new international treaty.[11] He specifically noted that "[The world's governments] came together in 1949 in Geneva Switzerland and that is what led to the recognition that they needed the fourth Geneva Convention to protect civilians in times of war. Now it the time for us to call on governments to protect civilians on the internet in times of peace."[12] In calling for a new "Digital

---

[8] Smith, *supra* note 1. In making this comment, Smith seemed to marginalized or discount responses to State cyber-attacks by the government of the victim State. He specifically stated that [i]nstead of nation-state attacks being met by responses from other nation-states, they are being met by us."

[9] *Id.*

[10] *Id.* With regard to this point, Smith was not only advocating better computer hygiene, individually and collectively, but also new computer security tools and better organizational structures and response capabilities.

[11] *Id.*

[12] *Id.* The entire list of proposals for the Digital Geneva Convention can be found at 11:43 of the video. They include: "1. No targeting of tech companies, private sector or critical infrastructure; 2. Assist

Geneva Convention," he pointed out that there have already been international cooperative efforts, both bi-laterally and multi-laterally, to establish new sets of norms.[13]   In the context of the Digital Geneva Convention, he also advocated for the establishment of an independent organization, like the International Atomic Energy Agency[14] which has addressed issues related to nuclear proliferation, to bring together the best and brightest from the private and public sectors as well as academia.[15] The purpose of this new international organization would be to not only observe what is happening in cyberspace between and among States, but also to identify attackers.[16]

Smith's third idea is that the global technology sector must become a trusted and neutral "Digital Switzerland" on which everyone can rely. This proposal is rooted, in part, in the significant role the International Committee of the Red Cross (ICRC) plays in the protection of the victims of armed conflict.[17] More specifically, the ICRC is an independent, neutral organization that ensures humanitarian protection and assistance for victims of armed conflict and other

---

private sector efforts to detect, contain, respond to and recover from events; 3. Report vulnerabilities to vendors rather than to stockpile, sell or exploit them; 4. Exercise restraint in developing cyber weapons and ensure that any developed are limited, precise and not reusable; 5. Commit to nonproliferation activities to cyber weapons; 6. Limit offensive operations to avoid a mass event.

[13] *Id.*

[14] *See* International Atomic Energy Agency (IAEA), *Official Web Site of the IAEA International Atomic Energy Agency (IAEA)*, https://www.iaea.org/ (last visited Aug 8, 2017).

[15] Smith, *supra* note 1.

[16] *Id.*

[17] *See* International Committee of the Red Cross, *International Committee of the Red Cross*, https://www.icrc.org/en (last visited Aug 8, 2017).

situations of violence.[18] It also promotes respect for the law of armed conflict and its implementation in national law.[19] In his speech, Smith draws parallels between the potential role and contributions of the global technology sector and the ICRC in terms of dealing with cyber security threats from States.

Smith is absolutely correct that there is an increasing threat of State cyber-attacks. In some cases, the cyberattacks happened in the context of an armed conflict while at other times the operations occurred during peacetime. For example, there was a Russian cyber campaign against Georgia immediately before and during their 2008 armed conflict whereby so-called Russian patriot hackers targeted Georgian government and news websites with Distributed Denial of Service (DDoS) attacks.[20] In 2010, the so-called Stuxnet worm was reportedly launched against Iranian uranium-enrichment centrifuges causing some of them to speed up thereby destroying them.[21] More recently, there were the so-called WannaCry and Peyta ransomware attacks which crippled hundreds of thousands of computers worldwide with the perpetrators of the attacks demanding digital ransom from the machines owners to regain access.[22] Last, but certainly not least, is the alleged Russian cyber

---

[18] *Id.*

[19] *Id.*

[20] SHAKARIAN, PAULO, JANA SHAKARIAN, ANDREW RUEF & SUSHIL JAJODIA. INTRODUCTION TO CYBER-WARFARE A MULTIDISCIPLINARY APPROACH, 24 (2013).

[21] BENJAMIN WITTES & GABRIELLA BLUM, THE FUTURE OF VIOLENCE: ROBOTS AND GERMS, HACKERS AND DRONES: CONFRONTING A NEW AGE OF THREAT 23 (2017).

[22] Nicole Perlroth, Mark Scott & Sheera Frenkel, *Cyberattack Hits Ukraine Then Spreads Internationally*, The New York Times (June 27, 2017), https://www.nytimes.com/2017/06/27/technology/ransomware-hackers.html (last visited Aug 7, 2017).

operation against the U.S. electoral system.[23]

Smith is not the only one that has called for a Digital Geneva Convention.[24] But given that he is the President of Microsoft Corporation; that there has been a spate of recent cyber operations by State actors or their proxies; and that increasingly more States are developing sophisticated cyber conflict capabilities, Smith's remarks exploded across the Internet. Moreover, the visceral appeal for such a cyber-specific treaty is greatly enhanced when linked to the 1949 Geneva Conventions, which are the most or one of the most well-known and highly regarded treaties in the history of humankind.[25]

This article will focus on Smith's proposal for a Digital Geneva Convention and, to a lesser extent, on his ideas for the establishment of an international, independent watchdog agency like the International Atomic Energy Agency and for the global technology sector becoming a trusted and neutral Digital Switzerland. Smith's speech should be viewed as an important step towards the improved rule of law in cyber operations, and a step that one hopes will continue to fruition. Smith's proposal, however, was made to a forum of technology experts and not to the international and legal community which is currently working on these issues. As such, it overlooks the significant work that has

---

[23] Michael Riley & Jordan Robertson, *Russian Cyber Hacks on U.S. Electoral System Far Wider Than Previously Known,* Bloomberg (June 13, 2017), https://www.bloomberg.com/news/articles/2017-06-13/russian-breach-of-39-states-threatens-future-u-s-elections.

[24] Rachael Kalinyak, *Companies want a Digital Geneva Convention; researchers demur*, Defense News (July 18, 2017), http://www.defensenews.com/home/2017/07/18/companies-fighting-for-a-digital-geneva-convention-for-cybercrime/.

[25] GARY D. SOLIS, THE LAW OF ARMED CONFLICT: INTERNATIONAL HUMANITARIAN LAW IN WAR 88 (2d ed. 2016).

already been accomplished in this area, such as the drafting and publication of the 2017 *Tallinn Manual 2.0*, which is a restatement of the international law as it currently exists with respect to cyber by a group of international experts.[26] In addition, Smith's proposal frames certain issues and uses analogies in ways that do not match the legal framework developed to date. As an example, Smith calls for a Digital Geneva Convention, which is understandable given the ubiquity and broad acceptance of this treaty. However, in practice, his specific proposals track more closely with the prohibitions on the use of force found in the U.N. Charter. In addition, his proposal overlooks the key dynamics by which international law is created, particularly through the adoption of treaties and customary law--both of which require significant State buy-in due to the need for State consent to such legal provisions. As a result, Smith and the technology community will need to persuade States to view his proposals as being in their best interest.

This article is written to encourage greater dialogue between the technology community and the international law community to achieve common terms of reference and a common understanding of the legal and technological challenges posed by cyberspace and operations. The technology community as a whole, and Smith's proposals in particular, offer insights and potential methods by which the legal norms could be developed. The international law community has been working on challenges posed by cyber for some time and provides a significant foundation to build upon to reach consensus on the international law framework for cyber operations. This article will review the

---

[26] TALLINN MANUAL 2.0 ON THE INTERNATIONAL LAW APPLICABLE TO CYBER OPERATIONS 1 (Michael Schmitt ed., 2d ed 2017) [hereinafter TALLINN MANUAL 2.0].

international law framework currently governing cyber and analyze how it would apply to the attacks cited by Smith. It will next turn to the need for State buy-in and consent to the multi-lateral treaty framework proposed by Smith, which is currently not likely. Finally, the article will review how the technology sector could assist in the development of a more effective international law framework governing cyber operations.

I.   SMITH'S PROPOSAL IMPLIES A NORMATIVE VOID IN INTERNATIONAL LAW

   A.   *The Foundational Structure of International Law*

For the technology community to appreciate the process by which a Digital Geneva Convention would be formed, it must understand the dynamics of the international legal system. Generally speaking, public international law is a body of law which is legally binding on States in their sovereign capacity (and not private individuals) in their intercourse with each other.[27] However, one cannot appeal to the UN General Assembly or similar world super-legislature to enact Smith's proposal of a Digital Geneva Convention as binding international law. Instead, there are

---

[27] ROBERT KOLB & RICHARD HYDE, AN INTRODUCTION TO THE INTERNATIONAL LAW OF ARMED CONFLICT 5 (2010). It is important to note that States are not the only subjects of international law. Individuals and international organizations may also fall under the purview of international law. Additionally, public international law is distinguished from private international law in that the latter is the rules that are established or agreed upon by citizens of different nations who privately enter into transactions and that will govern in the event of a conflict.

other, slightly different legal sources to consider. The Statute of the International Court of Justice recognizes three primary sources of international law:

(a) "international conventions" [*e.g.*, treaties]
(b) "international custom, as evidence of a general practice accepted as law"
(c) "the general principles of law recognized by civilized nations"[28]

These sources reveal an important element of international law—consent. States generally must consent to a legal obligation before they are obligated to abide by it. Such was stated in the classic international law case, *S.S. Lotus*,[29] but it can be seen in the two primary sources of international law: treaties and custom. Treaties by their nature require states to explicitly consent to be bound by the treaty requirements.[30] Custom does the same, albeit indirectly—the international law of custom allows states to

---

[28] Statute of the International Court of Justice art. 38, June 26, 1945, 59 Stat. 1055 [hereinafter *Statute of the ICJ*]. The Statute also cites, as a "subsidiary means" to determine the law, "judicial decisions and the teaching of the most highly qualified publicists [scholars] of the various nations."

[29] S.S. Lotus (Fr. v. Turk.), 1927 P.C.I.J. (ser. A) No. 10 at para. 144 (Sept. 7). In this case, the Court famously noted: "International law governs relations between independent States. The rules of law binding upon States therefore emanate from their own free will as expressed in conventions or by usages generally accepted as expressing principles of law and established in order to regulate the relations between these co-existing independent communities or with a view to the achievement of common aims. Restrictions upon the independence of States cannot therefore be presumed." *Id.*

[30] *See* Vienna Convention on the Law of Treaties, arts. 11-16, May 23, 1969, 1155 U.N.T.S. 331 (specifying the means of a state to express its consent to be bound by a treaty).

be a "persistent objector" as binding customary law is formed.[31] As a result, when it comes to customary law, silence to a developing customary legal norm can be considered to be *de facto* consent. Viewed through the prism of law-making, public international law generally is a relatively primitive legal system.[32] There are no legal institutions that are comparable to national legislatures with the power to promulgate laws of general applicability and no executive to enforce existing laws, instead States must enforce international law amongst themselves as sovereign equals, unless enforcement power has been delegated to a supra-national governance and judicial bodies such as the European Union or International Criminal Court. As a result, public international law is not created, interpreted, and enforced though the kinds of institutions found in domestic legal systems. Accordingly, as a body of law, it has had to justify its legitimacy and reality over the centuries.[33] At the extreme, there are even some highly respected commentators who take and argue the position that international law is not law at all. Rather, it is a special kind of politics where States coordinate their efforts to maximize their interests.[34] This view of public international law is neither new nor novel.

Another critical aspect of the international law process is that it is self-enforcing. That is, States enforce

---

[31] INT'L LAW ASS'N, STATEMENT OF PRINCIPLES APPLICABLE TO THE FORMATION OF GENERAL CUSTOMARY INTERNATIONAL LAW, principle 15 (2000) [hereinafter ILA CUSTOMARY LAW PRINCIPLES].

[32] THOMAS BUERGENTHAL & HAROLD G. MAIER, PUBLIC INTERNATIONAL LAW IN A NUTSHELL 19 (1985).

[33] LORI FISLER DAMROSCH & SEAN D. MURPHY, INTERNATIONAL LAW: CASES AND MATERIALS 1 (6th ed. 2009).

[34] MARY ELLEN O'CONNELL, THE POWER AND PURPOSE OF INTERNATIONAL LAW: INSIGHTS FROM THE THEORY AND PRACTICE OF ENFORCEMENT 2 (2011).

international law amongst themselves as sovereign equals.[35] This is most commonly seen through the doctrines of countermeasures and retorsion. Countermeasures are measures taken by States that themselves violate international law but are justified because they are done in response to a violation of international law by the targeted State.[36] Retorsion is similar—they are unfriendly measures that do not violate international law taken to show disapproval of the target's violation of international law.[37] President Obama's expulsion of Russian diplomats in response to alleged Russian cyber operations during the 2016 election has been reasonably characterized as retorsion.[38] Additional enforcement measures, such as enforcement actions by an independent enforcement body, can only exist if States agree to them, much like if they must consent to a treaty obligation. Examples of enforcement bodies include, but are not limited to, the UN Security Council, which is authorized to take action in response to threats to international peace and security[39] or the International Criminal Court, in which States have agreed to jurisdiction for war crimes under certain circumstances.[40]

Although international law is often maligned or

---

[35] FISLER & MURPHY, *supra* note 33, at 1.

[36] Int'l Law Comm'm, Responsibility of States for Internationally Wrongful Acts, art. 22, GA Res. 56/83 annex, UN Doc. A/RES/56/83 (Dec. 12, 2001) [hereinafter, Articles on State Responsibility]. Much like the Tallinn Manual 2.0, these articles represent a restatement of customary international law by the International Law Commission.

[37] *Id.*, *chapeau* to Chapter II of Part 3, para. 3.

[38] Michael N. Schmitt, *Peacetime Cyber Responses and Wartime Cyber Operations Under International Law: An Analytical Vade Mecum*, 8 Har. Nat. Sec. J. 239, 258 (2017).

[39] UN Charter, art 39.

[40] Rome Statute of the International Criminal Court, art. 1, July 17, 1998, 2187 U.N.T.S. 90.

marginalized and most certainly has shortcomings, it is widely accepted that "almost all nations observe almost all principles of international law and almost all of their obligations almost all of the time."[41] Speaking on the value and importance of international law, law professor Mary Ellen O'Connell observed:

> International law has deficits, yet it persists as the single, generally accepted means to solve the world's problems. It is not religion or ideology that the world has in common, but international law. Through international law, diverse cultures can reach consensus about the moral normal that we will commonly live by. As a result, international law is uniquely situated to mitigate the problems of armed conflict, terrorism, human rights abuse, poverty, disease, and the destruction of the natural environment. It is the closest thing we have to a neutral vehicle for taking on the world's most complex issues and pressing problems.[42]

In short, international law is a constantly evolving set of legal norms that are commonly observed by States in their relations with one another that confer rights and impose obligations in both peace and wartime.[43]

---

[41] Louis Henkin, How Nations Behave: Law and Foreign Policy 47 (1979).

[42] O'Connell, *supra* note 34, at 14.

[43] Edward Collins, Jr., International Law in a Changing World: Cases, Documents, and Readings 2 (1970).

B. Current Regimes Affecting Cyber: Governing Treaty and Customary Law

This section will examine the current international law provisions affecting cyber. Throughout Smith's talk, he implied that a normative legal void exists regarding cyber-attacks conducted by States. As will be seen below, this is not the case. In fact, there is extensive international law that applies and, in fact, many of the cyber-attacks that Smith cites are prohibited under international law. This section will outline the legal framework and then apply it to the cyber-attacks noted in Smith's talk. Ultimately, what will be seen is that the inherent weakness of the international law enforcement framework combined with the problem of attribution limits strong enforcement of the current existing law, resulting in a perception of a normative legal void in this area. As noted above, much of international law is comprised of customary law and there have been several attempts to restate current customary law as it applies to cyber, which shed helpful light on the current state of the law.[44]

---

[44] In the arena of customary law, it is common for academic and government experts to distill current state practice into statements of governing customary law. As noted by the Supreme Court, "where there is no treaty and no controlling executive or legislative act or judicial decision, resort must be had to the customs and usages of civilized nations, and, as evidence of these, to the works of jurists and commentators who by years of labor, research, and experience have made themselves peculiarly well acquainted with the subjects of which they treat. Such works are resorted to by judicial tribunals, not for the speculations of their authors concerning what the law ought to be, but for trustworthy evidence of what the law really is." *The Pacquete Habana,* 175 U.S. 677, 700 (1900).

1. Tallinn Manual/GGE Processes

The previous explanation of the international law development process provides a foundation for the work of experts to distill the international legal provisions currently in effect and apply them to the challenges posed by cyberspace and operations. This process is not unusual to the law, as lawyers frequently use existing legal frameworks and doctrines and extend them, by analogy, to novel subject areas such as the international regulation of emerging technologies. While a debate exists as to feasibility of extending current legal doctrine to cyberspace and operations, this is the starting point, at a minimum.

With respect to the Tallinn process, in 2009, the NATO Cooperative Cyber Defence Centre of Excellence (CCD COE), a renowned cyber research and training institution in Tallinn, Estonia, invited a group of experts to produce a manual on the international law governing cyber warfare.[45] This project brought together a distinguished group of international law scholars and practitioners to explore and articulate how extant legal norms apply to cyber warfare.[46] Namely, the experts examined both treaty provisions that may be extended to cyberspace and operations and whether current state practice has solidified to the point that it may be considered customary international law. Although much of international law is thought of as treaty law, customary law still plays an important role in developing and binding States.[47] Customary international law is defined as a general practice

---

[45] TALLINN MANUAL ON THE INTERNATIONAL LAW APPLICABLE TO CYBER OPERATIONS 1 (Michael Schmitt ed. 2013) [hereinafter TALLINN MANUAL].

[46] *Id.*

[47] A.P.V. ROGERS, LAW ON THE BATTLEFIELD 2 (2004).

of law under Article 38(1)(b) of the Statute of the International Court of Justice, which States follow out of a sense of legal obligation.[48] Put in a slightly different manner, customary international law results from the general and consistent practice of States that is followed by them from a sense of legal obligation.[49] Customary international law is binding on all States except in those circumstances in which a state consistently and unequivocally refused to accept a customary practice.[50]

In 2013, the *Tallinn Manual on International Law Applicable to Cyber Warfare* was published and released.[51] As a result of the success of this first Tallinn Manual, the NATO CCD COE initiated a follow-on project to expand the scope of coverage with an updated manual to include the international law governing cyber activities during peacetime as well as wartime. The NATO CCD COE convened a second group of international experts for the follow-on effort.[52] Their dedicated work led to the creation and publication of *Tallinn Manual 2.0* in 2017.[53] The significantly expanded Manual not only incorporated and updated the materials from the first Tallinn Manual, but also included coverage of legal regimes implicated by peacetime cyber activities and incidents.[54] Impressively, *Tallinn Manual 2.0* has 154 unanimously agreed upon rules with

---

[48] *Statute of the ICJ, supra* note 28.

[49] Theodor Meron, *Customary Law, in* CRIMES OF WAR 2.0 WHAT THE PUBLIC SHOULD KNOW, 141 (Roy Gutman, David Rieff, & Anthony Dworkin, eds., 2007).

[50] ADAM ROBERTS & RICHARD GUELFF, DOCUMENTS ON THE LAWS OF WAR 7 (3rd ed. 2000).

[51] TALLINN MANUAL, *supra* note 45.

[52] TALLINN MANUAL 2.0, *supra* note 26, at 1.

[53] *Id.*

[54] *Id.*

detailed commentary accompanying each rule which not only offers some tremendously important insights into the deliberations and thought processes of the experts regarding the legal basis and justification for the rules and their normative context, but also offers practical implications of the rules' application in a cyber context. This level of detail is particularly helpful for national legal advisors and academics. Additionally, the commentaries to the rules articulate positions by the experts in their discussions such that it is makes clear when either the experts all reached agreement or when they could not reach consensus on a specific issue.

Despite the great helpfulness of *Tallinn Manual 2.0*, its limitations must also be noted. It is important to reiterate that the experts were limiting themselves to a restatement of the *lex lata*, *i.e.*, the law as it exists, and avoided including statements reflecting the *lex ferenda*, *i.e.*, what the law should be.[55] Given the ephemeral process of determining customary law, the Tallinn process was not an unusual activity for international law experts, as they will frequently summarize current state practice and opinio juris to determine the law as it really is.[56] In addition, the *Tallinn Manual 2.0* clearly indicates that this effort was intended to be an expression of the opinions of the experts as to the current state of the law and is not an official document.[57] Despite this fact, the robust framework of the 154 rules unanimously agreed to by the international group of experts is strong evidence of the evolution of customary law that has taken place to address cyber operations. As a result, it can hardly be said that there is a legal normative void regarding

---

[55] *Id* at 3.
[56] *The Pacquete Habana,* 175 U.S. at 700.
[57] TALLINN MANUAL 2.0, *supra* note 45, at 2.

cyberspace and operations. In fact, as will be detailed later, each of the cyber operations Mr. Smith cited in his speech are addressed in the legal framework articulated in *Tallinn Manual 2.0*.

An important part of the process of creating *Tallinn Manual 2.0* was the so-called "Hague Process" hosted by the Netherlands Ministry of Foreign Affairs.[58] The Dutch convened States to unofficially comment on working drafts of *Tallinn Manual 2.0*.[59] Over 50 States and international organizations participated in the process in a Chatham House environment in three two day sessions.[60] Additionally, some States provided unofficial written feedback on the working drafts of *Tallinn Manual 2.0*, which led to a refinement of the text.[61] There was no such Hague process used with the first Tallinn Manual. Such collaborative interest and input for *Tallinn Manual 2.0* highlights how well regarded and received the Tallinn Manuals and process are for the international community. In addition to the Hague Process, the United Nations also attempted to facilitate discussions on cyberspace and operations between and among States. They did this through the UN Group of Governmental Experts on Developments in the Field of Information and Telecommunications in the Context of International Security (otherwise known as the Group of Governmental Experts, or GGE).[62]

The GGE is a UN-mandated working group

---

[58] *Id.* at 6.

[59] *Id.*

[60] *Id.*

[61] *Id.*

[62] Michael Schmitt & Liis Vihul, *International Cyber Law Politicized: The UN GGE's Failure to Advance Cyber Norms*, Just Security (June 30, 2017), https://www.justsecurity.org/42768/international-cyber-law-politicized-gges-failure-advance-cyber-norms/.

consisting of representatives from interested States focused on information security. The GGE process was established to create ongoing dialogue and consensus among States regarding the implications of the new technologies and the building of an international framework to promote security and stability with respect to information technology.[63] Until mid-2017, the GGE had achieved modest success, issuing two reports outlining principles on which there was consensus—an important starting point for the development of customary law.[64] Progress on this front has since stalled due to a breakdown in consensus.[65] Prior to this point there had been some progress, progress which was even noted by Smith in his RSA talk.[66] Notwithstanding the obvious disappointment at the GGE's failure to advance international cyber norms through inter-State discussions in 2017, it is encouraging that some progress has been made over the past five years through the promotion and development of cyber customary law like the Tallinn Manuals, the Hague process, and two earlier GGE reports. As will be discussed in greater detail below, the collapse of the GGE process speaks volumes about the difficulties of attaining the broad

---

[63] G.A. Res. 66/24, para. 4, A/RES/66/24 (Dec. 2, 2011).

[64] U.N. Group of Governmental Experts, Rep., transmitted by letter dated June 26, 2015, by the Chair of the group established pursuant to G.A. Res. 66/24 (2011), concerning Developments in the Field of Information and Telecommunications in the Context of International Security, para. 13, U.N. Doc A/70/174 (July 25, 2015)[hereinafter GGE 2015 report]; U.N. Group of Governmental Experts, Rep., transmitted by letter dated June 7, 2013, by the Chair of the group established pursuant to G.A. Res. 66/24 (2011), concerning Developments in the Field of Information and Telecommunications in the Context of International Security, paras. 19-25, U.N. Doc A/68/98 (June 24, 2013)[hereinafter GGE 2013 report].

[65] Schmitt & Vihul, *supra* note 62.

[66] Smith, *supra* note 1.

agreement necessary to establish a multilateral treaty like a Digital Geneva Convention and how some States would prefer confusion over legal norms in cyberspace operations to preserve their relative freedom of action in the digital domain.[67]

With this context, we can now turn to how current treaty and customary law applies to cyber operations. The most clear application is found in the Law of Armed Conflict. As noted in the *Tallinn Manual 2.0*, "[a]s with other operations, the law of armed conflict applies to cyber operations undertaken in the content of an armed conflict. Despite the novelty of cyber operations and the absence of specific rules within the law of armed conflict explicitly dealing with them, the experts were unanimous in finding that the law of armed conflict applies to such activities during both international and non-international armed conflicts."[68] This conclusion is significant because the 1949 Geneva Conventions, which will be discussed in detail below, are the single most important treaties comprising the law of armed conflict and is the centerpiece of Mr. Smith's proposal. This assessment that existing international law applies to cyberspace operations has been acknowledged by NATO, two GGE reports in 2013 and 2015 and by most States.[69] Additionally, the International Court of Justice confirmed in its *Nuclear Weapons Advisory opinion* that the UN Charter's Article 2(4) prohibition on the use of force and Article 51's recognition of an inherent right of self-defense

---

[67] Robert McLaughlin & Michael Schmitt, *The need for clarity in international cyber law*, Policy Forum (Sept. 18, 2017), https://www.policyforum.net/the-need-for-clarity-in-international-cyber-law/.
[68] TALLINN MANUAL 2.0, *supra* note 45, r.80, para.1.
[69] *Id.*

apply regardless of the weapon used.[70]

2. *Jus in Bello*: Law of Armed Conflict

The four Geneva Conventions of 1949 are at the foundation of the law of armed conflict.[71] The Geneva Conventions of 1949 are the most well-known and important treaties comprising the law of armed conflict. They are the most ratified international agreements in history.[72] All of the

---

[70] Legality of the Threat or Use of Nuclear Weapons, Advisory Opinion, 1996 I.C.J. 226, para. 39 (July 8) [hereinafter Nuclear Weapons Opinion].

[71] SOLIS, *supra* note 25, at 88.

[72] *Id.* The origin of the Geneva Conventions and the birth of the International Committee of the Red Cross can be traced back to 19th Century warfare and the efforts of a young Swiss businessman, Henri Dunant. Traveling on business in northern Italy, Dunant witnessed the battle of Solferino and its aftermath. The battle of Solferino was fought alongside the Mincio River in the Lombardy region of the country. This June 1859 battle of approximately 300,000 men involved the French, allied to the Sardinians facing, the Austrian troops. In its wake, 6,000 men were killed and 40,000 were wounded. Dunant was horrified by the carnage and the sight of abandoned and untended wounded which was the military practice at the time. Along with local residents and other volunteers, Dunant cared for the wounded and dying for three days and nights. Dunant was so moved by this experienced, he self-published a small book, *A Memory of Solferino*. The book not only graphically depicted the brutality and unspeakable misery of warfare at that time, but also called for a plan of action – a proposal. Dunant advocated the formation of relief societies to care for wartime wounded – the future International Committee of the Red Cross. Additionally, he called for the adoption of an intentional convention which ultimately resulted in the adoption of the first Geneva Convention in 1864. This convention provided principles that called for relief to wounded without distinction as to nationality; neutrality of medical personnel and establishments and units; and the distinctive sign or protective emblem of the red cross on white background. International Committee of the Red Cross, *From the*

nations of the world have ratified the conventions.[73] Given their universal acceptance, it is not at all surprising that Smith used the conventions as a benchmark for the regulation of cyber armed conflict. Fundamentally, the Geneva Conventions of 1949 are aimed at limiting the barbarity of armed conflict and protecting the following categories of war victims respectively: wounded and sick on land, the wounded, sick, and shipwrecked at sea, prisoners of war and civilians. There were a number of important innovations represented in the Geneva Conventions of 1949. First, there was, for the first time, a requirement that States enact domestic legislation to prosecute those who committed grave breaches of the Conventions.[74] Second, ratifying States were obligated to search out and try individuals who committed grave breaches.[75] Third, and a related point to the initial two innovations, the category of grave breach was included in the Conventions.[76] Finally, Common Article 3 was incorporated in all four conventions thereby providing baseline humanitarian protections in non-international

---

battle of Solferino to the eve of the First World War, (Dec. 28, 2004), https://www.icrc.org/eng/resources/documents/misc/57jnvp.htm.

[73] SOLIS, *supra* note 25, at 88.

[74] Geneva Convention for the Amelioration of the Condition of the Wounded and Sick in Armed Forces in the Field art. 49, Aug. 12, 1949, 75 U.N.T.S. 31 [hereinafter GCI]; Geneva Convention for the Amelioration of the Condition of Wounded, Sick and Shipwrecked Members of Armed Forces at Sea art. 50, Aug. 12, 1949, 75 U.N.T.S. 85 [hereinafter GCII]; Geneva Convention relative to the Treatment of Prisoners of War art. 129, Aug. 12, 1949, 75 U.N.T.S. 135 [hereinafter GCIII]; Geneva Convention relative to the Protection of Civilian Persons in Time of War art. 146, Aug. 12, 1949, 75 U.N.T.S. 287 [hereinafter GCIV].

[75] *Id.*

[76] GCI, *supra* note 74, art. 50; GCII, *supra* note 74, art. 51; GCIII, *supra* note 74, art. 130; GCIV, *supra* note 74, art. 147.

armed conflicts.[77] After the adoption of the Geneva Conventions in of 1949, they were supplemented by two Additional Protocols in 1977 to address developments in the conduct of warfare, specifically addressing guerrilla-type internal armed conflicts and revolutionary movements that had become the norm.[78]

The *Tallinn Manual 2.0's* experts were unanimous in their opinion that the law of armed conflict (primarily codified in the Geneva Conventions and the Additional Protocols) applied to "cyber operations executed in the context of an armed conflict."[79] Their opinion was based in part on the statement of the International Court of Justice in the *Nuclear Weapons* advisory opinion, indicated that the law of armed conflict applies "to all forms of warfare, and to all kinds of weapons, those of the past, those of the present, and those of the future."[80] The *Tallinn Manual 2.0* ultimately specified 70 rules drawn from the law of armed conflict which govern cyber operations taking place during armed conflict.[81] While one of the areas of disagreement leading to the breakdown of the 2017 GGE was whether the law of armed conflict applied,[82] one would be hard pressed to say that the law of armed conflict does not apply to cyber operations in armed conflict.

---

[77] SOLIS, *supra* note 25, at 87-118.

[78] GARY D. SOLIS & FREDERIC L. BORCH, GENEVA CONVENTIONS 33 (2010).

[79] TALLINN MANUAL 2.0, *supra* note 26, r. 80 & para. 1.

[80] *Id.* at 451, para. 1, citing Nuclear Weapons Opinion, *supra* note 70, para. 86.

[81] *Id.*, r. 80-149.

[82] *See* notes 150-158, *infra*, and accompanying text.

3. Jus ad Bellum

To a lesser degree and more indirectly, Smith's proposals implicate a second body of international law that regulates the international use of force – *jus ad bellum*.[83] Both *jus in bello* (discussed above) and *jus ad bellum* involve the regulation of the use of force, but in separate and distinct ways. That is, the laws comprising a State's right to wage war and the rights and obligations that are triggered once war has started unequivocally operate as distinct normative universes.[84] Accordingly, *jus ad bellum* means the right to resort to force or right to wage war.[85] It defines the legitimate reasons a State may resort to an armed conflict.[86] The primary modern legal authority underpinning modern *jus ad bellum* is the United Nations Charter, which addresses the concept in two key provisions. The first is Article 2(4) which provides that "[a]ll members shall refrain in their international relations from threat or the use of force against the territorial integrity or political independence of any State, or in any other manner inconsistent with the purpose of the United Nations."[87] By prohibiting the use of force,

---

[83] C. Stahn, *Jus ad bellum, jus in bello . . . jus post bellum? -Rethinking the Conception of the Law of Armed Force*, 17 Eur. J. of Int'l Law 921, 922 (2006). Some commentators believe that this traditional dualist conception of the laws of war should be extended to a third period following hostilities namely *jus post bellum*. This third period would involve the regulation of the ending of conflicts and easing the transition to peace through certain the application of norm. *Id.*

[84] INGRID DETTER DE LUPIS FRANKOPAN, THE LAW OF WAR 156 (2000).

[85] KOLB & HYDE, *supra* Note 27, at 9.

[86] *What are jus ad bellum and jus in bello?*, INTERNAT'L COMMITTEE OF THE RED CROSS (Jan. 22, 2015), https://www.icrc.org/en/document/what-are-jus-ad-bellum-and-jus-bello-0 (last visited Aug 15, 2017).

[87] UN Charter art. 2, para. 4.

rather than the somewhat anachronistic term war, the drafters of the Charter sought to avoid the debate about whether a particular conflict amounted to a war.[88] Leading scholars believe that the use of force between States is prohibited by a peremptory rule of international law.[89] The other provision is Article 51 of the United Nations Charter. It provides that "[n]othing in the present Charter shall impair the inherent right of individual and collective self-defense if an armed attack occurs against a Member of the United Nations."[90] The *jus ad bellum* fundamentally seeks to constrain the resort to force between states.[91] The *Tallinn Manual 2.0* extends these rules to cyber operations,[92] specifying that a cyber operation is a use of force "when its scale and effects are comparable to non-cyber operations rising to the level of a use of force."[93]

4. Sovereignty/Unlawful Intervention

Even though a cyber-attack might not be severe enough to qualify as a use of force or armed attack, less-

---

[88] THE HANDBOOK OF INTERNATIONAL HUMANITARIAN LAW 1 (Dieter Fleck, ed., 2nd ed, 2008).

[89] MARCO SASSOLI, *Jus ad Bellum and Jus in Bello – The Separation between the Legality of the Use of Force and Humanitarian Rules to Be Respected in Warfare: Crucial or Undated*, in INTERNATIONAL LAW AND ARMED CONFLICT: EXPLORING THE FAULTLINES, 241, 242 (Michael Schmitt & Jelena Pejic eds., 2007).

[90] UN Charter, *supra* note 87, art. 51.

[91] *IHL and other legal regimes – jus ad bellum and jus in bello*, INTERNAT'L COMMITTEE OF THE RED CROSS (Oct., 29, 2010), https://www.icrc.org/eng/war-and-law/ihl-other-legal-regmies/jus-in-bello-jus-ad-bellum/overview-jus-ad-bellum-jus-in-bello.htm (last visited Jan. 24, 2018).

[92] TALLINN MANUAL 2.0, *supra* note 45, r.68.

[93] *Id.,* r.69.

severe operations might still violate international law as a violation of sovereignty or an unlawful intervention in the affairs of another state. The protection of sovereignty is noted in Rule 4 of *Tallinn 2.0*, which provides as follows: "[a] State must not conduct cyber operations that violate the sovereignty of another State."[94] The Tallinn Manuals' experts did not precisely delineate when a cyber operation would constitute a violation of sovereignty. At a minimum, a violation of sovereignty would occur when "when one State's cyber operation interferes with or usurps the inherently governmental functions of another State."[95] In addition, sufficient "infringement upon the target State's territorial integrity"[96] would also qualify. While the degree necessary to constitute a sufficient infringement upon territorial integrity was not specified, the experts identified three levels of possible infringement: "(1) physical damage; (2) loss of functionality; and (3) infringement upon territorial integrity falling below the threshold of loss of functionality."[97]

The rule against intervention in the internal or external affairs of another State provides clearer contours and is considered a more serious violation of international law. Codified in the *Tallinn Manual 2.0*, Rule 66 states: "[a] State may not intervene, including by cyber means, in the external or internal affairs of another state."[98] The experts identified this rule as being based on the principle of sovereignty and Articles 2(1), (3) and (4) of the UN Charter.[99] This rule carves out a *domaine réservé* left "solely

---

[94] *Id.*, r. 4.

[95] *Id.*, r.4, para. 15.

[96] *Id.*, r. 4, para. 10.

[97] *Id.*, r. 4, para. 11.

[98] *Id.*, r.66.

[99] *Id.*, r. 66, para. 1.

to the prerogative of States" and "regarded as protected from intervention by other States"[100] The most frequently cited formulation of the *domaine réservé* is "choice of a political, economic, social and cultural system, and the formulation of foreign policy."[101] Cyber-attacks which intrude on a nation-state's *domaine réservé* would violate international law.

5. Conclusion

The above overview of both customary and treaty law demonstrates that significant work has been done and that a comprehensive international legal framework for cyber operations is currently in place. While challenges remain in governing this arena, they certainly are not due to a lack of legal provisions. That said, it is understandable that Smith might imply that a normative legal void exists necessitating a Digital Geneva Convention because of the number of cyber-attacks attributed to State actors as well as those acting as proxies for States. A review of the cyber operations cited by Smith will demonstrate both that there are substantive international law norms addressing these situations but will also begin to reveal the difficulties in of enforcing that law.

C. Prominent Attacks and Attacks Ccited by Smith—How They Fit into the Legal Framework

In his prelude to his proposal for a Digital Geneva Convention, Smith cited four instances of State cyber

---

[100] *Id.*, r.66, para. 7.
[101] Case Concerning Military and Paramilitary Activities in and Against Nicaragua (Nicar. V. U.S.), 1986 I.C.J. 14, para. 205 (June 27) [hereinafter *Nicaragua Judgement*].

operations: (1) the alleged Chinese theft of U.S. commercial secrets by Chinese military officers;[102] (2) the North Korean hack of Sony;[103] (3) the Russian takedown of the Ukraine power grid;[104] and (4) the Russian influence of the U.S. 2016 presidential elections through the release of information damaging to Hillary Clinton in the DNC emails and John Podesta emails which they had hacked.[105] Of these incidents, only the Chinese hack is not already prohibited by international law, although individuals engaged in the hack were indicted for violating the U.S. domestic law. We will look at each incident in turn:[106]

1. Sony/North Korea

The Sony cyber operation by North Korean proxy resulted in the deletion of significant amounts of data and the

---

[102] Pierre Thomas & Mike Levine, *US Charges 5 Chinese Military Hackers in '21ˢᵗ Century Burglary,'* ABCNEWS (May 19, 2014), http://abcnews.go.com/US/us-charges-chinese-military-hackers-21st-century-burglary/story?id=23774172. Smith showed this webpage on his slides while discussing this attack.

[103] Nakashima, Timber & Peterson, *supra* note 4.

[104] Jordan Robertson & Michael Riley, *How Hackers Took Down a Power Grid*, BLOOMBERG.COM (Jan. 14, 2016, 3:13 PM), https://www.bloomberg.com/news/articles/2016-01-14/how-hackers-took-down-a-power-grid. Smith showed this webpage on his slides while discussing this attack.

[105] *The John Podesta emails released by WikiLeaks*, CBS NEWS (Oct. 13, 2016, 4:42 PM), https://www.cbsnews.com/news/the-john-podesta-emails-released-by-wikileaks/. Smith showed this webpage on his slides while discussing this attack.

[106] Note that this analysis assumes that the attribution for the attack is correct, which is not necessarily a valid assumption. After a review of these hacks and the associated legal analysis, the following section will consider the difficulties that attribution poses to enforcing the existing legal regimes.

release of private information.[107] The data deletion and release of private information would also likely violate the sovereignty of the U.S. There are a couple of other points that should be made regarding this incident. The editor of the *Tallinn Manual 2.0*, Professor Michael Schmitt, indicated that such an operation, assuming that it could be attributed to the North Korean government, would in fact constitute a violation of U.S. sovereignty.[108] He would view the North Korean "manipulation of cyber infrastructure in another State's territory" and "the emplacement of malware within systems located [in another State]" as violations of the target State's sovereignty, and North Korea would be responsible for this internationally wrongful act."[109]

2. Russia/Podesta/DNC

In these two related instances, emails from both Jon Podesta and the Democratic National Committee which were damaging to the campaign of Hillary Clinton were released during the run-up to the 2016 U.S. presidential election. It appears that Podesta and the DNC were victims of a phishing email, which enabled malware to be downloaded to obtain the emails. While the emails were released through Wikileaks, the Obama administration publically attributed the operations to Russia and took measures in response to the attack, alleging that they were "intended to interfere with the US election process."[110] In

---

[107] Nakashima, Timber & Peterson, *supra* note 4.

[108] Michael Schmitt, *International Law and Cyber Attacks: Sony v. North Korea*, Just Security, (Dec. 17, 2014), https://www.justsecurity.org/18460/international-humanitarian-law-cyber-attacks-sony-v-north-korea/.

[109] *Id.*

[110] Press Release, Joint Statement of the Dept. of Homeland Sec. and

this instance, the hack appears to violate the prohibition on non-intervention in the affairs of another state, which is identified in Rule 66 of *Tallinn Manual 2.0*. This Rule implicates the concept of *domaine réservé*, those areas left "solely to the prerogative of States,"[111] of which elections would certainly qualify.[112] Note however, that the Obama Administration engaged in a "studied avoidance" on whether this cyber operation violated international law,[113] although an administration attorney indicated that a cyber operation that "manipulates another country's election results would be a clear violation of the rule of non-intervention."[114] While no reason was given for this "studied avoidance," Professor Schmitt indicated that the reason was to avoid a comparable characterization of similar U.S. cyber operations.[115] Despite the Obama Administration reluctance on this point, the administration allegation that Russian intended to influence the U.S. election would seem to imply that Russia violated the rule against non-intervention.

3. Russian Takedown of Ukraine Power Grid

In this situation, Ukrainian power stations were taken

Off. of the Dir. Of Nat'l Intelligence on Election Security, (Oct. 7, 2016), https://www.dhs.gov/news/2016/10/07/joint-statement-department-homeland-security-and-office-director-national.

[111] TALLINN MANUAL 2.0, *supra* note 45, r.66, para. 7.

[112] *See id.*, r.66, para. 2 (citing an operation to alter electronic ballots as an example of a violation of the prohibition against non-intervention).

[113] Ryan Goodman, *International Law and the US Response to the Russian Election Interference*, JUST SECURITY (Jan. 5, 2017), https://www.justsecurity.org/35999/international-law-response-russian-election-interference/.

[114] *Id.* (quoting State Department Legal Advisor Brian Egan).

[115] Schmitt, *supra* note 38, at 242-43 n. 5.

offline by an apparent hack by the Russian government or one of its non-State proxies.[116] This operation on the electrical grid is just one of numerous attacks that Ukraine has suffered over the past three years, which have systematically undermined every aspect of Ukrainian society.[117] These attacks appear connected with the current undeclared military conflict that is ongoing between Russia and the Ukraine, during which apparently Russian troops have facilitated the takeover of Crimea.[118] The general thought is that Russia is trying to undermine the credibility of the Ukrainian government.[119]

This particular conflict demonstrates again the applicability of international law, but also the difficulty of attribution and enforcement. To the extent that the military actions in the Ukraine are attributable to Russia (which seems quite clear), Russia is in violation of the UN Charter's prohibition on the use of force and these accompanying cyber operations would also constitute a violation of the prohibition on the use of force.[120] In fact, Professor Schmitt has noted that Russia is deliberately obfuscating its role in order to take advantage of "grey zones" in international law.[121] In addition, to the extent that the ongoing conflict is considered an international armed conflict (which is the

---

[116] Robertson and Riley, *supra* note 104.

[117] Andy Greenberg, *How an Entire Nation Becamse Russia's Test Lab for Cyberwar,* WIRED (June 20, 2017, 6:00 AM), https://www.wired.com/story/russian-hackers-attack-ukraine/.

[118] *Id.*

[119] *Id.*

[120] Thomas Grant, *Russia's Invasion of Ukraine: What does International Law have to Say?,* LAWFARE (Aug. 25, 2015, 7:45 AM), https://www.lawfareblog.com/russias-invasion-ukraine-what-does-international-law-have-say.

[121] Michael Schmitt, *Grey Zones in the International Law of Cyberspace*, 42 Yale J. of Int'l L. 1 (2017).

position of Amnesty International[122]), these cyber-attacks would also be regulated by the Geneva Conventions. While a belligerent is authorized to target a dual-use facility (that is, a facility with both a civilian and military purpose),[123] such as the electrical power grid, such an attack must offer the party a definite military advantage and, in addition, the attack must be proportional—that is, the collateral damage must not be excessive in relation to the expected military advantage.[124] In this particular case, assuming an international armed conflict, if in fact Russia is targeting electrical facilities to undermine the Ukrainian government, such an attack would likely be prohibited under the law of armed conflict as this does not constitute a definite military advantage.

4.   Chinese Hacking of U.S. Companies

The Chinese hacking of U.S. companies in order to engage in commercial espionage might not be unlawful under current international law, although it would certainly be a violation of U.S. domestic law. According to the article cited by Smith, the U.S. indicted five Chinese military officers for breaking into commercial networks and stealing secrets from U.S. nuclear, solar and metals industries.[125] This event was characterized by U.S. government officials as cyber espionage.[126] Rule 32 of *Tallinn 2.0* indicates that

---

[122] *Ukraine: Mounting evidence of war crimes and Russian involvement*, AMNESTY INTERNAT'L (Sept. 7, 2014, 00:00 UTC), https://www.amnesty.org/en/latest/news/2014/09/ukraine-mounting-evidence-war-crimes-and-russian-involvement/.

[123] TALLINN MANUAL 2.0, *supra* note 45, r.101.

[124] *Id.*, r. 113

[125] Thomas & Levine, *supra* note 102.

[126] *See id.* (quoting Assistant Attorney General for National Security

cyber espionage "does not *per se* violate international law" although the method utilized to conduct espionage might violate international law.[127] In this situation, where there appears to be little adverse effect beyond the pilferage of commercial secrets, it is likely that this attack would not violate current international law. That said, as noted by Smith in his speech, the United States and China entered into a bilateral agreement not to engage in commercial cyber espionage.[128] As a result, subsequent actions might constitute a violation of this agreement.

D. A significant part of the problem: attribution

The foregoing discussion overlooks a glaring problem preventing a strong enforcement regime for violations of international law in cyberspace—the attribution of who conducted the attack. The inability to definitively attribute an attack to a particular State renders it difficult or impossible to even engage the limited enforcement mechanisms available under international law. This attribution problem has several aspects: (1) How does one definitively determine the individual or computer

---

John Carlin indicating that this theft is cyber espionage).

[127] TALLINN MANUAL 2.0, *supra* note 45, r.32.

[128] Smith, *supra* note 1. This agreement was noted in a White House press release. The substance of the agreement stated: "The United States and China agree that neither country's government will conduct or knowingly support cyber-enabled theft of intellectual property, including trade secrets or other confidential business information, with the intent of providing competitive advantages to companies or commercial sectors." Press Release, The White House, *Fact Sheet: President Xi Jinping's State Visit to the United States*, (Sept. 25, 2015), https://obamawhitehouse.archives.gov/the-press-office/2015/09/25/fact-sheet-president-xi-jinpings-state-visit-united-states.

responsible for a particular attack?; (2) Even if one definitively identifies the individual responsible for an attack, how does one determine that the individual is operating on behalf of a State?; and (3) Even if a victim of a cyber-attack is able to definitively attribute the source of the attack to a State, how does the victim State provide proof of this fact without revealing its cyber and/or intelligence capabilities?

       1. Determining the individual or system responsible.

The nature of the Internet renders this determination very difficult in practice. This fact is highlighted by the comments by then-candidate Trump about "somebody sitting on their bed who weighs 400 pounds" who could be responsible for the alleged Russian election interference hacks.[129] Addressing this concern implicates the privacy debate that has been ongoing for some time. In fact, many in the technology sector laud developments that enable individuals to remain anonymous, such as encryption and anonymous browsing on the TOR router. Features such as these allows individuals to organize and communicate without government interference—a good thing for the Arab Spring, not so much for child pornographers and terrorists. In the U.S. there has been a strong resistance from the technology sector to proposals to require encryption backdoors which would allow the government to decrypt and

---

[129] This statement was made during the first Presidential debate against Hillary Clinton. *See* Aaron Blake, *The first Trump-Clinton presidential debate transcript, annotated,* THE FIX (Sept. 26, 2016), https://www.washingtonpost.com/news/the-fix/wp/2016/09/26/the-first-trump-clinton-presidential-debate-transcript-annotated/?utm_term=.def6b520e2a2.

view any encrypted communication.[130] However, tools enabling privacy and confidentiality also make it very difficult for governments to identify individuals conducting cyber-attacks.

The privacy debate is an important one, and we do not mean to suggest that all privacy protections should be abolished in order to solve the attribution problem. Instead, the technology sector should consider the effects that privacy-friendly policies have on their fight against State-sponsored cyber operations. A Digital Geneva Convention would be toothless if States continue to be able deflect claims of responsibility because no single entity can be effectively identified as the source of a cyber operation.

2. Attributing an attack to a State

Even if a victim of a cyber-attack is able to identify the individual or group perpetrating the attack, the State from which the attacker operated is not necessarily responsible. If the individual is operating on his/her own, without direction, control, or at the instruction of a State, then international law is not necessarily implicated. The *Tallinn Manual 2.0* lays out circumstances when an attack may be attributed to a nation-state, and two are particularly relevant to this inquiry: (1) "Cyber operations conducted by organs of a State, or by persons or entities empowered by domestic law to exercise elements of governmental authority";[131] (2) "Cyber operations conducted by a non-State actor" when either "engaged in pursuant to [the State's] instructions or under its

---

[130] Emblematic of this approach was Apple's refusal to comply with an FBI subpoena to decrypt the cell phone from the San Bernardino shooters. *See* Tim Cook, *A Message to Our Customers*, (Feb. 16, 2016), https://www.apple.com/customer-letter/.

[131] TALLINN MANUAL 2.0, *supra* note 45, r.15.

direction or control" or "the State acknowledges and adopts the operation as its own."[132]

If no conditions exist from which one may legally attribute an individual or group's cyber-attack to a State, [133] then the individual may be liable for violating the law in either the State from which he is operating or the target state being attacked. Such an individual can be prosecuted under the host State's laws or extradited to the victim state for prosecution. However, even the extradition process is difficult as States may refuse to extradite, as Russia has done for many Russian hackers indicted in the United States for violations of the Computer Fraud and Abuse Act.[134]

3. Proving an attack

The previous two hurdles are significant, but assuming they can be surmounted, then the victim of a cyber operation must be able to demonstrate attribution in order to credibly invoke the enforcement mechanisms that international law provides. A State may not be willing to do

---

[132] *Id.*, r.17.

[133] In addition to the possibility of formal attribution, a nation-state has a due diligence requirement to prevent cyber-attacks from cyber infrastructure within its borders or under its sovereign control. This requirement, however, is limited to requiring a state to take action to stop a cyber-attack when it has actual knowledge of the attack. Under this framework, a victim state must notify the state from which the attack is emanating and this state must take steps to stop the attack, otherwise the nation-state from which the attack is emanating is in violation of its international law due diligence obligations. *See* TALLINN MANUAL 2.0, *supra* note 45, r.4.

[134] Tim Lister and Tomas Etzler, *The US and Russia are fighting over the extradition of this hacking mastermind,* CNN (Nov. 26, 2017, 10:21 AM), http://www.cnn.com/2017/11/25/europe/us-russia-extradition-fight/index.html.

so, given that such an action may reveal that State's cyber capacities. International law does account for this difficulty, to a limited extent, in its rules permitting action in self-defense or countermeasures. States utilizing countermeasures need only utilize a reasonableness determination in order to execute countermeasures, but they are responsible for countermeasures that are made on a mistaken basis of attribution.[135] A similar reasonableness requirement exists for actions taken in self-defense.[136] That said, a State will likely desire to state its case to the international community, as the FBI did in attributing the Sony hack to North Korea.[137]

The attribution problem presents an opportunity for the technology sector to provide its expertise and develop a reputation as a trusted neutral party. The technology sector can analyze its data on attacks, in conjunction with information that States are willing to provide it, and make independent attribution assessments. To the extent that they would be able to build and retain a reputation for trustworthiness and neutrality, they could provide important input to the process and improve the ability of States to enforce the current legal framework. In addition, such a process might work in the long run towards States being willing to agree to a multilateral treaty regime that Smith proposes.

---

[135] TALLINN MANUAL 2.0, *supra* note 45, r.20, para. 15.

[136] *Id.,* r.71, para. 23.

[137] Press Release, FBI National Press Office, Update on Sony Investigation (Dec. 19, 2014), https://www.fbi.gov/news/pressrel/press-releases/update-on-sony-investigation .

II.   STATES ARE UNLIKELY TO AGREE TO SMITH'S PROPOSED
       DGC WHICH LIMITS THEIR CYBER OPERATIONS

Notwithstanding the fact that there are significant international law provisions applicable to cyber operations, there is another critical point that Smith must consider when seeking to achieve the goal of a Digital Geneva Convention: will States agree to join and abide by such a treaty? In the case of the UN Charter and the Geneva Conventions, States affirmatively agreed to join these multi-lateral treaties and give their provisions legal effect. These "laws" were not imposed by a super-legislature of States, nor by some other outside authority. To the extent that custom also developed over time, States could be persistent objectors to a developing custom and the State would not be legally bound.[138]

This raises a key question: Why do States agree to legal obligations in the first place? There are many scholarly theories and discussions on why a State agrees to assume a legal obligation, but the issue boils down to whether a State views the assumption of such an obligation as being in its best interest.[139] That is, the prospective perceived benefits of joining the treaty regime must outweigh the perceived costs of assuming the legal obligation.

The fundamental problem, then, that Smith faces is that he has to be able to persuade the States that are allegedly using cyberspace to conduct operations—Russia, China, United States, Israel, Iran, and North Korea among many others—to agree to substantial limits on their ability to

---

[138] *See* ILA CUSTOMARY LAW PRINCIPLES, *supra* note 31, principle 15. This principle provides that "[i]f whilst a practice is developing into a rule of general law, a State persistently and openly dissents from the rule, it will not be bound by it." *Id.*

[139] MARK WESTON JANIS, INTERNATIONAL LAW, 12-14 (5th ed., 2008).

conduct cyber operations. In order to do so, Smith has to be able to answer a number of questions:

> -Why is it in these States' best interest to agree to these limits?
> -How can they be assured that others will comply? How can a State be reasonably certain that other States will comply especially considering the highly secretive nature of cyber operations as well as the fundamental problem of attribution? As a corollary, how would these legal provisions be enforced?
> -How can these legal provisions be enforced when it's so difficult to attribute a cyber operation to a particular State?

Smith and other proponents of the Digital Geneva Convention fail to answer the question of why it would be in the best interest of the States to agree to such legal restrictions. In fact, Professor Schmitt argues that the opposite is occurring—that States are taking advantage of "grey zones" in international law in order to conduct cyber operations.[140] Before addressing the issue of consent as it applies to cyber, it will be helpful to consider why States agreed to the *jus in bello* and *jus ad bellum* codified in the Geneva Conventions and UN Charter respectively. From this starting point, we can examine the potential reasons for States to agree to additional significant legal restrictions and obligations. This article will now turn to examine the origins of these bodies of law to help answer that question.

---

[140] Schmitt, *supra* note 121, at 2-3.

A. Consent and the Geneva Conventions and UN Charter

When examining the origins of the Geneva Conventions and UN Charter, it is important to keep in mind that they were adopted shortly after the world experienced the horrors of the Second World War and the commencement of the nuclear age. In fact, the 1949 Geneva Conventions represent the first time in modern history an international treaty has achieved universal acceptance,[141] whereby all States in the world agree to the protections it affords to the victims of war. Similarly, the UN Charter's prohibition on the use of force and the *jus ad bellum* framework have been widely accepted, to the extent that the International Court of Justice has stated that it constitutes customary law.[142] While World War Two may have served as the impetus for the adoption of these treaties, there are several reasons why it is within a State's best interest to adhere to these legal bodies of law.

From a practical point of view, compliance with the law of armed conflict promotes military effectiveness. For example, pursuant to the Third and Fourth Geneva Conventions, States involved in an international armed conflict are to treat prisoners of war and protected persons humanely and in accordance with the obligations detailed within those two conventions.[143] The practical effect of this

---

[141] Press Release, Internat'l Committee of the Red Cross, Geneva Conventions of 1949 achieve universal acceptance, (Aug. 21, 2006), https://www.icrc.org/eng/resources/documents/news-release/2009-and-earlier/geneva-conventions-news-210806.htm.

[142] *Nicaragua Judgement, supra* note 101, para. 188.

[143] Under the Fourth Geneva Convention, article 4, protected persons are defined as follows: "[p]ersons protected by the Convention are those who, at a given moment and in any manner whatsoever, find

is twofold: (1) Members of the respective armed forces will not feel compelled to "fight to the death" because they will be confident that they will be treated humanely upon capture by their adversary; (2) it will ultimately be easier for the parties to the conflict to end the hostilities. The reverse of this is also true. If during an armed conflict, the parties to the conflict intentionally violate the law of armed conflict by doing things like -- targeting civilians and civilian objects, or mistreating prisoners of war and protected persons – it will likely prolong a conflict.

Compliance with the law of armed conflict also increases the likelihood of reciprocity among nations. If one party to an armed conflict abides by the laws of armed conflict, it may serve to encourage or facilitate their adversaries to act in the same or similar way. Of course, there is not a guarantee this will happen. It is also important to note that the law of armed conflict is not based upon reciprocity. Common article one to the 1949 Geneva Conventions provides "[t]he High Contracting Parties undertake to respect and to ensure respect for the present Convention in all circumstances." Put in a slightly different manner, States are required to comply with their obligations regardless of what their adversaries do. But, as a practical matter, if you treat the other side's prisoners inhumanely and target civilians and civilian objects, one cannot be too surprised if

---

themselves, in case of a conflict or occupation, in the hands of a Party to the conflict or Occupying Power of which they are not nationals. Nationals of a State which is not bound by the Convention are not protected by it. Nationals of a neutral State who find themselves in the territory of a belligerent State, and nationals of a co-belligerent State, shall not be regarded as protected persons while the State of which they are nationals has normal diplomatic representation in the State in whose hands they are." Geneva Convention relative to the Protection of Civilian Persons in Time of War art. 4, Aug. 12, 1949, 75 U.N.T.S. 287

the other side does the same or similar things.

Also, there is a significant reputational cost for failing to comply with both the law of armed conflict and the *jus ad bellum*, both internationally and domestically. One need only think about incidents of Abu Gharib or the My Lai massacre. The loss of legitimacy associated with engaging in such conduct has practical consequences. For example, after 9/11, organs and agents of the United States mistreated a number of the prisoners it held in the so-called war on terrorism. Some of this maltreatment included the actual torture of prisoners. Unquestionably, this conduct stained the reputation of the United States and its armed forces and intelligence agencies. The practical effect of such conduct is that it made other countries, in some cases, reluctant to operate with the United States. Also, as a practical matter, it makes it very difficult to prosecute individuals that were physically and mentally coerced or otherwise subject to torture or cruel, inhumane, or degrading treatment. This type of conduct undermines the position of the United States internationally especially from a morality or rule of law perspective. With respect to the impact domestically, violations of the law of armed conflict undermine a war effort. It helps galvanize support against involvement in an armed conflict. Again, the massacre at My Lai during the Vietnam War is an example of an incident that helped erode domestic public support for the conflict.

From a humanitarian perspective, armed conflict is not intended to be a bloodsport. In fact, the modern law of armed conflict has largely been driven by humanitarian concerns and pressures.[144] As noted by Professor Gary Solis, "[t]he idea of war as indiscriminate violence suggests violence as an end in itself, and that is antithetical to the fact

---

[144] SOLIS, *supra* note 25, at 8.

that war is a goal-oriented activity directed to attaining political objectives."[145] Additionally, war victims on all sides of a conflict are not responsible for the fact that their State decided to fight an armed conflict.[146] Even from a humanitarian perspective, it is important to highlight that the law of armed conflict is a body of law that, even at its very best, is never more than imperfectly observed and, at its worse, is very poorly observed.[147] Commenting on the laws regulating warfare, British historian Geoffrey Best stated "[i]ts mission, strictly speaking, is impossible. It seeks to introduce moderation and restrain into a medium peculiarly insusceptible to those qualities."[148] Coming full circle, States agree to the Geneva Conventions and the use of force prohibitions contained in the U.N. Charter to mitigate the harshness and brutality of warfare. That is, the law of armed conflict "has done nothing but good, and the implication is clear, that wars where it was not enforced, known, or even dimly apprehended, were the most horrible for their lack of it."[149]

B. Breakdown of Government Group of Experts Process: Not a Good Start

The prospects of developing a universally-accepted Digital Geneva Conventions were significantly diminished by the recent actions of the UN Government Group of Experts (hereafter GGE).[150] The breakdown or collapse of

---

[145] *Id.*

[146] MARCO SASSƆLI, ANTOINE A. BOUVIER & ANNE QUINTIN, HOW DOES LAW PROTECT IN WAR? 119 (2011).

[147] GEOFFREY BEST, HUMANITY IN WARFARE 11 (1980).

[148] *Id.*

[149] *Id.* at 12.

[150] Schmitt & Vihul, *supra* note 62.

the processes was generally along Cold War lines with States like Cuba, Russia and China rejecting the final report due to three additions to a list of cyber-relevant legal principles and rules that had been originally agreed to by the experts in 2015.[151] Specifically, these nations objected to statements affirming States' ability to act in self-defense in cyberspace and to utilize countermeasures in response to internationally wrongful acts committed in cyberspace.[152] Finally, these nations objected to a statement affirming the applicability of the law of armed conflict in cyberspace.[153] Unlike the universally agreed-upon norms protecting the victims of war espoused in the 1949 Geneva Conventions, it is hard to ignore the fact that, as noted by Professor Schmitt and Liis Vihul, even well-accepted international legal norms have been intentionally politicized.[154] It is not entirely clear why Cuba, Russia, and China took such untenable political positions on the above issues even though they have accepted the general applicability of international law to cyberspace and operations.[155] Schmitt and Vihul have speculated that their positions may be rooted in a desire to avoid the perception that the "the West" is disproportionally prescribing the principles and the rules governing cyberspace.[156] Alternatively, these recalcitrant States, particularly Russian and China, may be viewing their position through a legal-operational lens of wanting to deprive the United States and its Western allies of a legal justification for responding to their hostile cyber

---

[151] *Id.*

[152] *Id.*

[153] *Id.*

[154] *Id.*

[155] *Id.*

[156] *Id.*

operations.[157] Finally, "opposition to acknowledging basic and irrefutable legal notions may reflect the current dismal state of relations outside the cyber realm. These may be 'softball' legal issues, but right now everyone is playing 'hard ball.'"[158]

The dynamics –legal, political, and practical-- underpinning the failure of the U.N. GGE powerfully illustrate why the notion of reaching broad international consensus on a Digital Geneva Convention for Cyberwarfare is not only infeasible but highly unlikely. Some of the most direct fault lines and frictions between States exist in the cyber domain. Is the United States going to forgive Russia for interfering in its 2016 elections? China has pillaged intellectual property from American companies through cyber espionage for decades resulting in the greatest transfer of wealth in human history.[159] It is difficult to overstate the negative impact that such theft has had on American economic growth and prosperity and the ways in which it has undermined America's military and national security.[160]

In addition and related to the intractable nature of the international and political dynamics mentioned above, as a practical matter, most of the States that are particularly advanced and active with cyber operations would not be interested in entering into a Digital Geneva Convention. Cyber operations are among the most sensitive, highly classified secrets held by States. In many respects, "[t]he entire phenomenon of cyber war is shrouded in such

---

[157] *Id.*

[158] *Id.*

[159] Dennis Blair & Keith Alexander, *China's Intellectual Property Theft Must Stop*, N.Y. TIMES (Aug. 15, 2017), https://www.nytimes.com/2017/08/15/opinion/china-us-intellectual-property-trump.html.

[160] *Id.*

government secrecy that it makes the Cold War look like a time of openness and transparency." [161] Unlike conventional and even nuclear weapons and warfare, everything related to cyber warfare in enveloped in extreme secrecy. [162] Not to overstate a point, there are certainly many aspects of nuclear weapons that are highly classified: specifics about design and capabilities; launch codes; targeting plans; and command and control among many other tactical, operational, and strategic details. [163] But, in comparison to cyber weapons, there is much that is publicly known and widely understood about nuclear weapons and warfare such as how many particular States have at any given time; how they generally work; and the terrifying reality of what happens when they are used. [164]

> C. *Proposal for a cyber International Atomic Energy Agency presumes a robust treaty regime for enforcement—might be helpful but still requires consent.*

Despite the difficulties identified above, there is merit to Mr. Smith's idea of an international, independent watchdog agency like the International Atomic Energy Agency (hereinafter IAEA). However, even such an organization requires State consent to a multi-lateral treaty. The IAEA is comprised of member States who have ratified the Statute of the IAEA, [165] a multi-lateral treaty establishing

---

[161] RICHARD A. CLARKE, CYBER WAR xi (2010).

[162] FRED KAPLAN, DARK TERRITORY: THE SECRET HISTORY OF CYBER WAR 284 (2016).

[163] *Id.*

[164] *Id.*

[165] Statute of the International Atomic Energy Agency, July 29, 1957, 276 U.N.T.S. 3 [hereinafter IAEA Statute].

the IAEA which 169 nation-states have ratified.[166] The IAEA Statute specifies the functions of the IAEA, which is primarily focused on research, development and safety in the development of peaceful uses of nuclear energy.[167] The IAEA is governed by the General Conference, comprised of all Member States, and the Board of Governors, which has a rotating membership of 35 Member States.[168] While much of the public face of the IAEA consists of the technical experts who conduct inspections and issue reports, it cannot be forgotten that their work is also overseen by the Member States to the Statute of the IAEA. In addition, it should be noted that the Statute of the IAEA does not address nuclear nonproliferation. This topic is addressed by the Treaty on The Non-Proliferation of Nuclear Weapons, which specifies that the IAEA will work with States subscribing to the Non-Proliferation Treaty to ensure that peaceful nuclear energy programs do not divert materials to developing nuclear weapons.[169] The work of the IAEA, then, is a verification mission, not an enforcement mission. Enforcement is left to States, usually working through the United Nations.

Smith's proposal of an IAEA-like structure might be a helpful first step in the process of more robust international law framework for cyber operations. Note that the Statute of the IAEA entered into force in 1957, fairly soon after the start of the nuclear age. While the dangers of nuclear

---

[166] *List of Member States,* IAEA, https://www.iaea.org/about/governance/list-of-member-states (last visited Jan. 19, 2018)

[167] *See* IAEA Statute, *supra* note 165, art.3 (specifying functions of the IAEA).

[168] *Id.,* arts. 5-6.

[169] *See* Treaty on the Non-proliferation of Nuclear Weapons, art. 3, July 1, 1968, 729 U.N.T.S. 161 [hereinafter Nuclear Non-proliferation Treaty].

weapons were clear at that time, this Statute did not attempt to address substantive issues such as non-proliferation and nuclear weapons disarmament, which would have been non-starters at that time.[170] Instead, the Statute focused on peaceful uses of nuclear energy and standards for nuclear safety.[171] This foundation allowed IAEA to assist in the implementation of the Non-Proliferation Treaty when it entered into force in 1970, overseeing the peaceful development of nuclear energy to ensure that nuclear materials were not then diverted to weapons development.[172] A similar process in the case of cyber might be to create a similar organization to promote peaceful development of the global network and promote safety and security. That said, while there is a clear demarcation between peaceful and non-peaceful uses of nuclear energy, there is not a similar clear-cut line in the cyber arena as the range of uses of cyberspace is much more varied than nuclear energy. Despite this fact, an independent agency that begins to analyze and discuss issues related to cyber security would be a helpful first step.

The bottom line conclusion in response to Smith's call for an "independent watchdog" akin to the IAEA, is that, much like the prospects of a multi-lateral treaty, States would have to consent to such an agency in order for it to have any enforcement teeth. Given the dynamics addressed earlier and the dim prospects of a widely-accepted multilateral treaty regarding cyber, a similar resistance by States should be expected in response to this proposal.

---

[170] *See* IAEA Statute, *supra* note 165, art.3 (specifying functions of the IAEA).arp

[171] *Id.*

[172] Nuclear Non-proliferation Treaty, *supra* note 169, art. 3.

III.   THE TECH SECTOR COULD ASSIST IN THE DEVELOPMENT
         OF INTERNATIONAL LAW AS IT APPLIES TO CYBER

>   *A.   Develop a reputation as a trusted agent—this*
>   *could serve as a platform for ongoing*
>   *discussion and debate on the development of*
>   *cyber operations law.*

In Smith's speech, he proposes that the technology sector serve as a "digital Switzerland," committed to 100% defense and 0% offense. This analogy might be a little inaccurate—the idea of a Switzerland conveys the picture of a neutral state in a belligerency, which implies an entity remaining "above the fray," studiously avoiding assisting any of the belligerent parties. By emphasizing the degree to which the technology sector is on the "front lines," Smith's digital Switzerland analogy begins to break down.

A better analogy might be to the International Committee of the Red Cross (ICRC). The ICRC has been a critical component to the development and functionality of the law of armed conflict. The ICRC was present at the adoption of the four Geneva Conventions and has enjoyed a unique status under the law.[173] Part of their effectiveness is due to the fact that the ICRC has developed a reputation as a trusted agent, working directly with all parties to a conflict with the goal of advancing the cause of humanity in warfare without regard to the identity of the parties involved.[174] This model might be a better model for the technology sector to

---

[173] GCI, *supra* note 74, art. 9; GCII, *supra* note 74, art. 9; GCIII, *supra* note 74, art. 9; GCIV, *supra* note 74, art. 10.

[174] *See Building Respect for the Law*, INT'L COMM. OF THE RED CROSS (Jan. 5, 2011), https://www.icrc.org/eng/what-we-do/building-respect-ihl/overview-building-respect-ihl.htm (noting their outreach efforts to military and police units and armed groups fighting their governments).

attempt to emulate. As noted in Smith's speech, the technology sector is on the front lines on a regular basis and, as a result, has a unique ability to provide a helpful perspective to shape the development of the law. With the right leadership, cooperation from the largest global technology leaders, and a good-faith commitment to eliminating the weaponization of the Internet, the technology sector could create an entity like the ICRC to engage in the discussion and promote its vision of the internet.

B. *Join the international law dialogue with a correct understanding of the state of the law and how international law is developed.*

As has been discussed much within this article, there are significant efforts to address the international law issues associated with cyberspace. However, these efforts are largely the product of government officials, military officials and academics, not technology industry leaders. To date, there has been minimal participation from technology industry leaders. For example, the *Tallinn Manual 2.0* seven-page list of International Group of Experts and Other Participants includes only one individual who is affiliated with the technology industry.[175] Similarly, the list of participants from the 2013 and 2015 UN GGE reports is also devoid of technology industry representatives.[176]

To address this void, the technology industry must inject itself into the process. They bring an expertise and front-line perspective that will help all parties understand the

---

[175] TALLINN MANUAL 2.0, *supra* note 45, at xviii. That individual is Jeffrey Carr, who is listed as being affiliated with Taia Global Inc.
[176] *See* 2015 GGE Report, *supra* note 64, annex; 2013 GGE Report, *supra* note 64, annex.

issues involved. However, instead of broad-brushed calls for a new treaty, the industry must appreciate the nuance and challenges presented by international law attempts to regulate this field. First, the industry must have an appreciation of the current state of customary law, as reflected by *Tallinn Manuals* and the GGE reports. Indeed, this lack of understanding is exposed by the fact that most of the cyber-attacks cited by Smith are addressed (albeit imperfectly) by the current legal framework. This understanding would lay the framework for progress on two additional fronts: (1) understanding the current "grey zones" in the law where the law does not adequately address the technological developments (and how some nation-states may use these grey-zones to their advantage); and (2) understanding the inherent limits of the enforceability of international law and the degree to which the lack of attribution renders the enforcement of the current legal framework even more difficult than normal. Second, the industry must have an appreciation of the degree to which the principle of state consent underlies the international law system. As stated earlier, to have a State sign a treaty limiting its options in cyberspace requires that the State view adopting the treaty as being in its national interest. Few States take this view as to date it is clear that States are taking advantage of gray zones to maximize flexibility in their cyber operations. Similarly, the development of customary law norms requires the same consideration, lest States reject developing customary norms as persistent objectors.

Part of the process that the technology sector can engage with is the development of customary law. While the authors of the Tallinn Manual were very careful to report on custom as it currently exists (*lex lata*, or existing law), and to avoid engaging in advocacy as to what the law should be (*lex ferenda*),[177] there is a place for advocacy of *lex ferenda* by outside organizations. This can result in the consequent adjustment of customary law as state practice shifts in response to such calls for such changes.[178] The technology sector is in an ideal position to engage in *lex ferenda* advocacy based on their unique perspective. Indeed, there are models for the technology industry to consider as they enter the field. There are accepted models of establishing new customary norms through indirect means such as the establishment of soft law norms.[179] For example, codes of best practices, industry standards or aspirational norms can be defined, which may be adopted by individuals, corporations and/or States.[180] Over time, such best-practices or standards may gain widespread acceptance among States to the point where they evolve beyond soft-law aspirational guidelines and are cemented as hard-law customary law.[181]

In fact, Smith's proposal for the technology sector pledge could be characterized as a soft law norm. Smith advocates that the global technology sector sign its own pledge to the following terms: 1. No assistance in offensive actions; 2. Collaborative proactive defense; 3. Collaborative remediation after attacks; 4. Software patches made available to all; 5. Coordinate disclosure practices for vulnerabilities; 6. Support for intergovernmental defensive

---

[177] *See supra* note 55, and accompanying text.

[178] GERHARD VON GLAHN AND JAMES LARRY TAULBEE, LAW AMONG NATIONS: AN INTRODUCTION TO PUBLIC INTERNATIONAL LAW, 44-46 (10th ed. 2013).

[179] *Id.* at 68-69.

[180] *Id.*

[181] *See,* D.J. Bederman, *Constructivism, Positivism, and Empiricism in International Law*, 89 Georgetown L. Rev. 469, 484 (reviewing ANTHONY CLARK AREND, LEGAL RULES AND INTERNATIONAL SOCIETY (2001)).

efforts.[182] Such a pledge, if carried out effectively, would be significant towards the beginning of a soft-law norm and also might assist in establishing the technological sector as a trusted agent in the process. The process of developing soft-law norms is generally time-consuming, indirect and not always successful, but would provide a real road-map to industry engagement in the development of customary norms for cyber operations.

IV.   CONCLUSION

Because companies like Microsoft and those similarly situated are on the front lines, as Brad Smith notes, it is understandable that they would perceive a significant problem from the increased number of State-sponsored cyber-attacks. Enforcement of international law is handicapped due to the difficulties discussed above and States taking advantage of gaps in the law in order to advance their national interests. It is understandable why Smith might perceive there to be a void in the legal framework, but this perception is not quite accurate. The international legal community should welcome the technology sector's involvement, and perhaps the joint efforts of these two groups working in concert might create a better functioning legal framework that meets the needs of States and the technology sector.

---

[182] Smith, *supra* note 1.

Does the Cryptographic Hashing of Passwords Qualify for Statutory Breach Notification Safe Harbor?

Jason R. Wool*

Data breaches are increasingly part of the news cycle, especially as "mega breaches" occur from time to time impacting tens of millions of people (two recent examples include OPM and Equifax). Today, 48 states have passed legislation requiring notifications to consumers (and sometimes regulators) following a data breach, in addition to several non-state jurisdictions like D.C. and Puerto Rico. In light of the ubiquity of these laws, those unfamiliar with data breach-related legal practice may be forgiven for assuming there is a rich body of case law interpreting state notification statutes. Surprisingly, however, there are very few cases analyzing the nuts and bolts of these laws, leaving some quirks in the various statutes to be analyzed by lawyers in a guidance vacuum.

Password hashing is one such mystery of state data breach notification law analysis. Every state with a breach notification law effectively provides an exemption from statutory breach notification requirements when breached "personal information" is encrypted and the encryption key

* *Jason Wool, CIPP/US, CIPP/E,* is Counsel at ZwillGen PLLC. Jason's practice focuses on information security, including cyber risk management, incident response, and compliance with global data protection laws, regulations, and standards, including the PCI-DSS. He holds a B.A. from Haverford College and a J.D. from William & Mary. The views expressed in this article are solely those of the author, and do not necessarily represent those of any organization with which the author may be associated.

remains secure (referred to as "safe harbor"). However, none of the jurisdictions that consider some form of a username and password to be personal information (and therefore potentially subject to data breach notification obligations) explicitly refer to password hashing in their statutes, even though most organizations hash, rather than encrypt, passwords.[1] Personal information, as defined in state breach notification statutes, has traditionally consisted of data such as social security numbers, driver's license numbers, and financial account numbers. This data would typically be encrypted rather than hashed as a data protection measure. But as user credential breaches become increasingly prevalent, some states have begun bringing this type of information in the scope of mandatory breach notification.

This article analyzes two under-explored aspects of password hashing in the context of state breach notification laws. First, it explores whether password hashing can qualify for data breach notification "safe harbor" provisions, which typically apply where data is encrypted. This article concludes that password hashing can generally qualify for safe harbor, but that the argument is more difficult to make in three of the states examined. Second, even if password hashing can qualify for safe harbor under these laws, it explores whether hashing always qualifies or if it does only when certain minimum criteria are met. This article concludes that minimum criteria must reasonably be met, given that some hashes are trivial to crack. The state breach notification laws do not provide much clarity on this point.

Ultimately, this article identifies as a statutory

---

[1] At the time of writing, at least eight jurisdictions – California, Florida, Illinois, Nebraska, Nevada, Puerto Rico, Rhode Island, and Wyoming – consider some form of a user ID and password to be "personal information."

shortcoming the fact that the state breach notification laws in jurisdictions that consider user credentials to be personal information do not always clearly acknowledge the reality that hashing is used to protect the data in question. Moreover, they also do not provide sufficient criteria for assessing the effectiveness of hashing with respect to determining the applicability of safe harbor provisions. As bulk user credential data breaches become more common, the lack of statutory clarity around hashing may give rise to significant uncertainty about when regulators consider notification under the state breach notification laws to be required for incidents involving account credentials.

I.   OVERVIEW OF BREACH NOTIFICATION LAWS AND SAFE HARBOR PROVISIONS

Breach   notification   laws   typically   require notification to individuals impacted by a data breach, as well as to regulators like state attorneys general in some cases. The laws typically define the set of data elements that can be subject to a data breach and usually call those data elements "personal information."[2] The statutes also typically define a data breach (or some similar term), often using language such as "unauthorized acquisition, or reasonable belief of unauthorized acquisition, of personal information that compromises the security, confidentiality, or integrity of the personal information maintained by the information collector."[3]

All breach notification statutes in the U.S. contain provisions clarifying that notification is not required if the data was protected in certain ways. These are sometimes

---

[2] *See, e.g.*, Alaska Stat. § 45.48.090(7) (2016).
[3] *Id.*

referred to as "safe harbor" provisions. There are a number of variations of the safe harbor provision in state breach notification laws, but they generally all apply to data that is encrypted regardless of the specific language used. In some cases safe harbor is provided explicitly where personal information that was subject to a data breach was encrypted and the encryption key was not compromised or stolen.[4] In some of these statutes, the term "encryption" is defined,[5] however, others do not define it.[6] Some statutes provide safe harbor but do not use the term encryption at all.[7] Other statutes provide safe harbor where personal information is encrypted, redacted, or otherwise rendered unreadable.[8] Regardless of the specific language used, encryption of personal data generally qualifies for safe harbor in the event of a data breach (assuming the key was not compromised or stolen).[9] But at least in some instances, other data protection mechanisms can also qualify for safe harbor. This is most obvious in those statutes that do not use the term encryption, or that also make reference to redaction or other measures that render personal information unreadable or unusable.[10]

---

[4] *See, e.g.*, N.Y. Gen. Bus. Law § 899-AA (2016) (defining "private information" as "personal information consisting of any information in combination with any one or more of the following data elements, when either the personal information or the data element *is not encrypted, or encrypted with an encryption key that has also been acquired*").

[5] *See, e.g.*, Ariz. Rev. Stat. § 18-545(L)(3) (2017).

[6] *See, e.g.*, Alaska Stat. § 45.48.090.

[7] *See* D.C. Code § 28- 3851(1) (2017) ("Acquisition of data that has been rendered secure, so as to be unusable by an unauthorized third party, shall not be deemed to be a breach of the security of the system.").

[8] *See, e.g.*, Wis. Stat. § 134.98(b) (2017).

[9] *See, e.g., supra* notes 4-8.

[10] *See, e.g., infra* note 53.

But even where safe harbor is only provided for encrypted data it is possible that other protection mechanisms can qualify, especially where the term "encryption" is defined broadly.

While encryption generally qualifies for safe harbor, encryption is not the same as hashing, nor are all hashing techniques equally secure. For the eight jurisdictions that consider a username and password, in some form, to constitute personal information, it is not always clear whether hashing qualifies for safe harbor, or, to the extent hashing *can* qualify for safe harbor, whether all or only some hashing processes can do so. Moreover, as discussed below, there are additional considerations with respect to an attacker's ability to crack passwords than the hash function used (i.e. the auxiliary hashing practices discussed in Section IV).

II.   OVERVIEW OF CRYPTOGRAPHIC HASHING

Because encryption is strongly associated with breach notification safe harbor provisions, and hashing is often mistakenly equated with encryption, it is important to highlight the key differences between the two. Understanding these differences, as well as some of the limitations of hashing, is critical to the discussion later in this article concerning whether hashing can qualify for safe harbor under state breach notification laws.

The National Institute of Standards and Technology ("NIST") defines encryption as the "conversion of plaintext to ciphertext through the use of a cryptographic algorithm."[11] Importantly, encryption is bi-directional – that

---

[11] Glossary of Key Information Security Terms, NISTIR 7298 at 69 (2013), http://nvlpubs.nist.gov/nistpubs/ir/2013/NIST.IR.7298r2.pdf.

is, through the operation of cryptographic processes, plaintext (such as the word "hat") can be turned into ciphertext (i.e., encrypted output), and then decrypted back into plaintext using the appropriate cryptographic key.[12] Encryption can be *symmetric*, meaning that the sender and recipient each have a key that both encrypts plaintext and decrypts ciphertext, while *asymmetric* (or "public key") encryption means that each party to a communication has a public key used to encrypt plaintext and a private key used do decrypt ciphertext.[13] Examples of popular encryption algorithms in wide use today are the Advanced Encryption Standard (AES) and the Rivest, Shamir, Adleman (RSA) algorithm.[14]

Hashing, unlike encryption, is intended to be a unidirectional transformation of plaintext (or a "preimage") into a hash value (also known as a "message digest").[15] Hashing algorithms take inputs of plaintext of an arbitrary length and produce alphanumeric digests or "hashes" of a fixed length.[16] For instance, the MD5 hash of "hat" is "46b5e59b2fd342bf8fee10c561958725," while the MD5 hash of "supercalifragilisticexpialidocious" is "08206e04e240edb96b7b6066ee1087af." Hashes are often used to represent sensitive data in a database so that the actual sensitive data does not itself need to be stored because hashes are not meant to be reversed and should, if effective,

---

(citing FIPS 185).

[12] *See id.* at 57 (defining cryptography, citing FIPS 191).

[13] *See id.*

[14]*E.g.*, OWASP, Cryptographic Storage Cheat Sheet at 2.1.2.1, (2017) https://www.owasp.org/index.php/Cryptographic_Storage_Cheat _Sheet.

[15] *See* NISTIR 7298, *supra* note 11 at 53 (defining "cryptographic hash function").

[16] *See id.*

create a unique digest for every input.[17] This is particularly useful where it is not actually important *what* the sensitive data is, such that restoring the original plaintext is unnecessary. For instance, hashes can be used to prove that two strings are the same without comparing the strings. Take passwords: when a password is first registered, a hash is generally created and stored in association with the username. When a user attempts to authenticate later, the password entered is run through the same hashing process and the digest is compared to the one on file. If they are the same, the user has, at least in theory, entered the correct password.[18] Hashes are used in many other contexts too, including to prove that a string or file has not changed over time, *i.e.* that it has retained its integrity, as doing so would result in a different digest.[19] They can also be used to identify

---

[17] *See id.* (noting that an *approved* cryptographic hash function must be one-way and collision resistant. NIST defines collision resistance as "an expected property of a hash function whereby it is computationally infeasible to find a collision," where "collision" is defined as "an event in which two different messages have the same message digest." Quynh Dang, *Recommendation for Applications Using Approved Hash Algorithms*, Special Publication 800-107 at 3 (2012)).

[18] Some hash functions are vulnerable to collisions, such as MD5 and SHA-1, meaning that two different inputs can result in the same hash. While collision vulnerabilities are beyond the scope of this article, it is important to note that hash functions are *intended* to create unique digests for all conceivable inputs. While collision vulnerabilities are cause for significant concern, they present less of a risk in the context of password hashing and more in the context of digital signatures, where the ability to trust that a digital signature is unique is integral to the ability to trust that the entity presenting that signature is, in fact, that entity.

[19] In theory, even a change of one byte in a plaintext input should result in a completely new and different ciphertext after being run through a hashing function. *See, e.g.*, KAREN KENT et al, GUIDE TO INTEGRATING FORENSIC TECHNIQUES INTO INCIDENT RESPONSE, Special Publication

a file or string. For instance, the hash of a photograph can be used to identify instances of that photograph in a data set.[20]

    Password hashing algorithms come in a wide variety of types, but we tend to assess their security using a small number of criteria. One of the primary criteria is slowness (also referred to as "expense").[21] Hash algorithms can compute hashes very quickly or slowly depending on their design and configuration. Although there are instances in which a fast hashing algorithm is desirable (such as for computing a hash for an entire disk image, or for creating a checksum to be used to verify the integrity of a file), when it comes to passwords it is desirable for a hashing algorithm to be slow, or expensive.[22] The reason for this is that if an attacker were to obtain the entire password table, we would want to reduce the number of guesses the attacker is able to make each second to the greatest extent possible. MD5 and SHA-1 are two popular hashing algorithms that are generally thought of as being *fast*.[23] On the other hand, bcrypt, and

---

800-86 at 4-8 (2006) (describing the use of hash functions to verify the integrity of copied data during forensic investigations).

[20] For instance, PhotoDNA is a technology that enables companies like Google to identify child pornography images in users' email and other accounts by comparing hashes of images stored in those accounts to "robust hashes" of known pornographic images. *See, e.g.,* Microsoft, "New Technology Fights Child Porn by Tracking Its 'PhotoDNA,'" (Dec. 15, 2009) https://news.microsoft.com/2009/12/15/new-technology-fights-child-porn-by-tracking-its-photodna.

[21] A related criterion is resistance to GPU attacks, discussed below.

[22] *See, e.g.,* NATIONAL INSTITUTE OF STANDARDS AND TECHNOLOGY (NIST), Special Publication 800-63B, DIGITAL IDENTITY GUIDELINES: AUTHENTICATION AND LIFECYCLE MANAGEMENT at 15 (2017) ("A memory-hard function SHOULD be used because it increases the cost of an attack.").

[23] *See, e.g.,* Automation Rhapsody, "MD5, SHA-1, SHA-256 and SHA-512 speed performance," (Oct. 23, 2017), https://automationrhapsody.com/md5-sha-1-sha-256-sha-512-speed-

PBKDF2 are generally thought of as being *slow*.[24] The slower the hashing algorithm, the more computationally expensive it is for the attacker and the less likely that the hashes will be subject to a brute force attack (in which all possible combinations of characters are attempted until the correct password is guessed) or other complex attacks.

III.   OVERVIEW OF PASSWORD CRACKING

This section reviews how password cracking works, as this practice illustrates the broad spectrum of (in)secure practices that can be used when creating hashes of passwords. Depending on how a password is hashed, it can be easily cracked in a fraction of a second, rendering the hashing pointless from a security perspective. On the other hand, some hashes could take years to crack, rendering them highly secure in the event of a breach. Accordingly, the type of hashing practices employed by an organization has a direct bearing on whether a particular data breach can qualify for safe harbor.

A full analysis of the current state, and the underlying mechanics, of password hash cracking is beyond the scope of this article.[25] However, some background information is necessary to inform the analysis of the state breach notification statutes discussed below. This article assumes

---

performance.

[24] *See, e.g.,* Bill's Security Site, "Hash Speed Test," https://asecuritysite.com/encryption/htest (last visited Jan. 23, 2018).

[25] For two very useful overviews of these topics, *see* Nate Anderson, "How I became a password cracker," ARS TECHNICA (Mar. 24, 2013), https://arstechnica.com/security/2013/03/how-i-became-a-password-cracker/, & Dan Goodin, "Why passwords have never been weaker—and crackers have never been stronger," ARS TECHNICA (Aug. 2, 2012), https://arstechnica.com/security/2012/08/passwords-under-assault/.

all password cracking would occur (1) offline and (2) in the context of a hacker obtaining an entire database of password hashes. This assumption is generally in line with today's website security practices. It is possible to attempt to crack passwords online, however security controls such as limiting the number of incorrect authentication attempts before an account becomes locked, CAPTCHA requirements, and forcing users to wait an increasingly long period of time between failed log-in attempts have become standards among websites, which prevents many of the attack types discussed below from being usable in this context.[26]

There are several popular methods of cracking password hashes, (*i.e.* of guessing the correct input plaintext and thereby replicating a given hash). Perhaps the most famous of these methods is brute force. While brute force attacks can be infeasible in many contexts, their utility depends in large part on the type and configuration of the hashing algorithm employed by the hash database's owner. For instance, in a 2012 article on the blog *Coding Horror*, the author described having a PC employing two graphics processor units (GPUs) – essentially hyper-powerful processing units designed to handle the intense graphical needs of some computer video games, which are quite popular among password cracking aficionados. Using this PC, the author could create all possible hashes for 6 character passwords hashed with standard MD5 and using uppercase and lowercase letters, numbers, and all possible symbols, in 47 seconds.[27] With only uppercase, lowercase, and numbers in the passwords, the PC in question could

---

[26] *See* Special Publication 800-63B, *supra* note 22 at 25-26 (discussing recommended controls to protect against online guessing attacks).

[27] Jeff Atwood, "Speed Hashing," *Coding Horror* (Apr. 6, 2012), https://blog.codinghorror.com/speed-hashing/.

create all possible hashes in 3 seconds.[28] As the minimum length and complexity of passwords increase, however, so does the time required to brute force the passwords. For example, the *Coding Horror* author noted at the time of writing that the time required to brute force all 8 character MD5 passwords required to use at least one each of uppercase, lowercase, numbers, and all possible symbols would take approximately 465 days.[29] The time this task would take has likely significantly decreased five years later, in accordance with Moore's law. Moreover, even in 2012 it was possible to create highly specialized, hyper-fast rigs designed specifically for password cracking that essentially daisy chain GPUs. Dan Goodin of *Ars Technica* described one such rig in 2012 that combined 25 GPUs and was capable of trying "180 billion combinations per second against the widely used MD5 algorithm."[30] Today, systems with high powered GPUs can be rented from Amazon Web Services, making these types of attacks more accessible.[31] These high powered, easily accessible systems also facilitate password-based attacks like reverse brute force attacks, also known as password spraying attacks, in which a single, commonly used password is used to attempt to authenticate to a large number of user accounts in fast succession.[32]

---

[28] *See id.*

[29] *See id.*

[30] Dan Goodin, "25-GPU cluster cracks every standard Windows password in <6 hours," ARS TECHNICA (Dec. 9, 2012), https://arstechnica.com/security/2012/12/25-gpu-cluster-cracks-every-standard-windows-password-in-6-hours/.

[31] *See, e.g.,* Rockfish Sec, "GPU Based Password Cracking with Amazon EC2 and oclHashcat,", Last accessed January 23, 2018 from: http://www.rockfishsec.com/2015/05/gpu-password-cracking-with-amazon-ec2.html.

[32] *See, e.g.,* Jacob Wilkin, "Simplifying Password Spraying," *SpiderLabs Blog*, https://www.trustwave.com/Resources/SpiderLabs-

The attack of choice for password crackers in most cases is the dictionary attack, in which a word list – often times a dictionary or list of passwords recovered from previous data breaches, such as the famed "rockyou.txt" file containing approximately 14.5 million unique preimage[33] passwords recovered from a 2009 data breach – is used to hash guessed combinations of words, numbers, and special characters using predefined rule sets until hashes are generated that match those in a particular hash table.[34] These types of attacks are often carried out using popular, easily accessible freeware such as HashCat and John the Ripper.[35] In years past, a specialized attack using a so-called "rainbow table," a massive, precomputed table for reversing cryptographic hash functions, was viewed as a particularly significant risk in the context of offline password cracking attacks. However, the expense of maintaining such enormous files (often in the range of terabytes in size), the increasing popularity of security features such as salts, and the increasing viability of hyper-fast, increasingly affordable dictionary attacks using daisy-chained GPUs has apparently brought this attack method out of fashion.

Blog/Simplifying-Password-Spraying/ (last visited Jan. 23, 2018).

[33] A preimage is defined as "a message X that produces a given message digest when it is processed by a hash function." NISTIR 7298, *supra* note 11 at 5.

[34] *See, e.g.,* ANDERSON, *supra* note 25.

[35] *See id.* These tools will inevitably become even more effective, especially when combined with technologies such as machine learning. *See, e.g.*, Briland Hitaj et al, "PassGAN: A Deep Learning Approach for Password Guessing," *arXiv*:1709.00440 at 2 (Sep. 1, 2017) (describing a method for replacing human-generated password rules with machine learning-generated ones, which when initially tested in combination with HashCat resulted in an 18-24% increase in effectiveness vis-à-vis HashCat alone).

Salts are strings of characters automatically appended to a plaintext password prior to hashing, which add additional complexity and randomness to input plaintext. They are often stored along with each password hash, as the salt used in combination with a plaintext password input is necessary whenever a user attempts authentication. Because the salt is generally randomly generated, sufficiently long (e.g., 128 bytes in bcrypt), and unique to each hash, rainbow tables are generally ineffective when salts are used. A salt that is stored separately from password hashes that is meant to be kept secret is sometimes referred to as a "pepper." NIST currently recommends the use of both a salt and a pepper when hashing passwords.[36]

Depending on the technically enforceable rules an organization has put in place with respect to password complexity, offline brute force and dictionary attacks executed through programs like HashCat generally result in *some* hashes being cracked in a large password hash database, regardless of the hash function used. This appears generally to be a function of the poor quality of the passwords that end up being cracked. For instance, passwords that utilize a word in combination with a number at the end – for example, "picnics7" – will often be trivial to crack because they use a dictionary word and fall under one of several classic password configurations (i.e. a word followed by a single digit, regardless of the hash function used). Even worse, some users employ passwords like "password" and "123456" that can be cracked in milliseconds, as they are among the 20 or so that are most commonly found in password hash tables.

---

[36] *See* National Institute of Standards and Technology (NIST), Special Publication 800-63B, *supra* note 22 at 15, *Digital Identity Guidelines: Authentication and Lifecycle Management* at 15 (2017).

Unless an organization prohibits and technically prevents the use of passwords that are dictionary words, appear on known word lists, conform to common patterns, are prone to brute force attacks (e.g., 000000), or otherwise are vulnerable to known cracking attacks, it is highly likely that if a password hash database is acquired by bad actors, some of the hashes will be cracked. NIST guidance provides that, prior to accepting a password, a verifier should compare it "against a list that contains values known to be commonly-used, expected, or compromised" including "passwords obtained from previous breach corpuses, dictionary words, repetitive or sequential characters (e.g. 'aaaaaa', '1234abcd'), [and] context-specific words, such as the name of the service, the username, and derivatives thereof."[37]

PBKDF2 and bcrypt are well regarded hash functions for passwords, in particular, because they are far less vulnerable (meaning they offer greater "preimage resistance") to attacks utilizing GPU daisy-chaining.[38] For instance, following Ashley Madison's highly publicized data breach in 2015, in which 36 million hashes were exfiltrated from Madison's servers, the owner of the famed 25-GPU cracking rig declined to even attempt to crack the hashes in the leaked table explicitly because Madison had used bcrypt.[39] Indeed, the owner of the specialized rig "estimated

---

[37] *Id.* at 14.

[38] Preimage resistance is defined as "an expected property of a hash function such that, given a randomly chosen message digest, *message_digest*, it is computationally infeasible to find a preimage of the *message_digest*. NISTIR 7298, *supra* note 11 at 5. Preimage resistance is "measured by the amount of work that would be needed to have a high probability of finding a preimage for a hash function." *Id.* at 7.

[39] Dan Goodin, "Lessons learned from cracking 4,000 Ashley Madison passwords," ARS TECHNICA (Aug. 26, 2015), https://arstechnica.com/security/2015/08/cracking-all-hacked-ashley-

it would take years using a highly specialized computer cluster just to check the dump for the top 10,000 most commonly used passwords."[40] Nonetheless, another researcher stepped in to try his hand at cracking some of the Ashley Madison password hashes, and "after five days of nonstop automated guessing using a moderately fast server specifically designed to carry out compute-intensive cryptographic operations, he deciphered just 4,000 of the underlying plaintext passwords."[41] Among the cracked passwords were "123456," "password, "12345," qwerty", and some explicit phrases. While 4000 cracked hashes over four days is generally disappointing for researchers in the context of a leak of more than 30 million leaked hashes, it is important to emphasize that even where one of the most highly recommended hashing functions is used, at least some leaked or stolen hashes are likely to be cracked in the immediate aftermath of a data breach unless the impacted organization has a particularly strong set of controls in place governing password construction.

There is at least one other potentially significant risk associated with password hashing that is sometimes overlooked in discussions of its use. While the use of an expensive hashing algorithm in combination with a strong password policy can be immensely helpful in combatting password cracking when a bad actor obtains an entire password table, their effectiveness may be reduced in some instances if an attacker is targeting a specific user. For instance, if an attacker combines social engineering or open source research on an individual known to be included in a password hash dump, he or she may be better able to crack

---

madison-passwords-could-take-a-lifetime/.
[40] *Id.*
[41] *Id.*

the single hash associated with that individual.[42] This risk is especially heightened where an individual uses the same password at multiple websites.[43] The common availability of password lists sourced from large scale data breaches facilitates attackers' ability to target individual users.[44]

IV.   SUMMARY OF KEY CONSIDERATIONS FOR SECURE PASSWORD HASHING

As the previous sections discussed, both hashing and encryption are cryptographic in nature, but they are not the same thing, and they have different use cases. The differences between encryption and hashing are important to understand from a policymaking perspective. Indeed, viewing the two as interchangeable could lead to breach notification statutes that offer protections to entities that

---

[42] For instance, in an August 2017 blog post, "the hacker known as 'Alex'" describes attempting to gain access to a friend's email account as part of an authorized white hat exercise using a multitude of publicly available resources and data, including social media and publicly available lists of passwords and password hashes associated with known data breaches, many of which can be researched using the well-intentioned https://haveibeenpwned.com. *See* The hacker known as "Alex," "Operation Luigi: How I hacked my friend without her noticing," https://defaultnamehere.tumblr.com/post/163734466355/operation-luigi-how-i-hacked-my-friend-without_(last visited Feb. 18, 2018).

[43] *See* Martin Bos, "Introduction to GPU Password Cracking: Owning the LinkedIn Password Dump," *Trusted Sec Update* (Jun. 17, 2016), https://www.trustedsec.com/june-2016/introduction-gpu-password-cracking-owning-linkedin-password-dump ("The LinkedIn list offers an opportunity for us . . . .[to] show how we attack large password breach lists. The passwords gained from these types of breaches are very valuable to us on penetration tests because people often reuse passwords across work and social media.").

[44] *Id.*

suffer data breaches in spite of their use of weak, easily cracked password hashes. This outcome would be contrary to the goals of breach notification statutes.

As discussed in the previous sections, it is apparent that the hash function that is used to hash passwords is a key consideration, and that the expensiveness of the function is a primary criterion for selecting a hash function. However, in addition to the function selected, there are a number of other practices that can be combined with the hash function to maximize the chances of protecting all hashed passwords in the event of a data breach. These include the use of an appropriate salt, the use of a pepper, and the use of password selection rules that prevent the use of passwords that are easy to guess, such as those found in known breach corpuses and the dictionary, or that would otherwise be easily cracked using programs like HashCat. This article will sometimes refer to these practices as "auxiliary hashing practices." Even if a strong hash function is used to hash passwords, a data breach involving password hashes that were not subject to most (if not all) of these auxiliary hashing practices is likely to lead to at least some of the password hashes being cracked.

V.   PASSWORD HASHES IN THE CONTEXT OF STATE BREACH
      NOTIFICATION REQUIREMENTS

As noted previously, there are several variations on breach notification safe harbor provisions, including those that refer to encryption, as well as those that refer to additional or alternative mechanisms for protecting data.[45] This Article focuses on the safe harbor provisions in the statutes of eight states that consider some form of a user ID

---

[45] *See supra* Section I.

and password to be "personal information."

In most contexts, safe harbor provisions in state breach notification statutes are sufficient for their intended purpose and will usually be satisfied using generally accepted types of encryption (e.g., AES 256). Most breach notification statutes are primarily concerned with breaches affecting data such as Social Security numbers and financial account numbers, which can be protected with encryption that easily meets the applicable statutory requirements. However, the same is not necessarily true for passwords, which are generally protected through hashing.

As described in greater detail below, the hashing of passwords at least arguably qualifies for safe harbor for purposes of the eight state breach notification statutes discussed in this article, although in some of the statutes the argument is more difficult to make. In fact, in some states the legislature may not have intended for password hashing to be subject to the special protections afforded to traditional encryption under the state breach notification laws. For instance, the Rhode Island statute refers to the "transformation of data through the use of a one hundred twenty-eight (128) bit or higher algorithmic process into a form in which there is a low probability of assigning meaning without use of a confidential process or key," which would only make sense in the context of a small subset of hash functions. When Rhode Island was in the process of amending its breach notification statute in 2015 to include this definition of encryption, several commenters pointed out to the legislature that the definition was overly narrow, but the legislature did not change the definition of encryption in response to these calls, which suggests that it did not agree with the commenters.[46]

---

[46] For instance, one trade association pointed out that "'128 bits' may

In some states, hashing may not *originally* have been intended to qualify for safe harbor, as the inclusion of usernames and passwords in the statutory definition of personal information occurred after the inclusion of a safe harbor provision.[47] For instance, Illinois had already included an encryption safe harbor provision when it passed HB1260, which added login credentials to the definition of "personal information," in 2016. [48] Nevada's statute also already provided safe harbor for encrypted data when it added login credentials to the definition of personal

---

not be possible or appropriate depending on the data and systems being utilized Letter from Laura Dooley, Auto Alliance, to the Honorable Brian Patrick Kennedy (Mar. 17, 2015), (on file with the author). Another commenter pointed out that the "exact method of encryption is less important than that the information is rendered unreadable or unusable, which is the standard used by many other states." Letter from James J. Halpert, State Privacy & Security Sec. Coal., Inc., to the Honorable Brian Patrick Kennedy (Mar. 17, 2015), (on file with the author).

[47] This is due to the nature of hashing and the traditional types of data sought to be protected by data breach notification laws. For example, Social Security numbers consist of nine digits and could therefore be relatively easy to brute force if hashed without using additional security measures. Driver's license numbers and credit card numbers would likely also be relatively easy to brute force if the pattern used were to be known, or if known prefixes, such as Bank Identification Numbers, were to be used. *See, e.g.,* Simson L. Garfinkel, "De-Identification of Personal Information," NISTIR 8053, at 17 (2015), https://nvlpubs.nist.gov/nistpubs/ir/2015/NIST.IR.8053.pdf (describing brute force attack against taxi medallion numbers that were hashed and publicly released in a dataset).

[48] *See* HB1260 (Ill. 2016), http://www.ilga.gov/legislation/publicacts/99/PDF/099-0503.pdf.

information in AB179 in 2015.[49] Nebraska[50] and Wyoming[51] also added user credentials to the definition of personal information after their current safe harbor provisions already existed in their respective statutes. Conversely, California added its current definition of encryption after it added user credentials to the definition of personal information.[52]

Regardless of the original legislative intent, several of the state breach notification statutes discussed below appear to implicitly acknowledge that hashing can qualify for safe harbor by providing a sufficiently broad exemption for notification that is not directly tied to encryption.[53] But even where hashing can in theory qualify for safe harbor, the question of whether it constitutes "encryption" or otherwise

---

[49] *See* A.B. 179 (Nev. 2015), http://www.leg.state.nv.us/Session/78th2015/Bills/AB/AB179_EN.pdf.
[50] *See* L.B. 835 (Neb. 2016), https://nebraskalegislature.gov/FloorDocs/104/PDF/Slip/LB835.pdf.
[51] *See* S. File 0036 (Wis. 2015), http://legisweb.state.wy.us/2015/Engross/SF0036.pdf.
[52] *See* S.B. 46 (Cal. 2013), https://leginfo.legislature.ca.gov/faces/billNavClient.xhtml?bill_id=201320140SB46 (adding user credentials to definition of personal information); A.B. 964 (Cal. 2015), https://leginfo.legislature.ca.gov/faces/billNavClient.xhtml?bill_id=201520160AB964 (defining encryption).
[53] See, e.g., Cal. Civ. Code § 1798.82 (2017) (defining the term "encryption"); Fla. Stat. § 501.171 (2017) (providing notification safe harbor for data that is "secured or modified by any other method or technology that removes elements that personally identify an individual or that otherwise renders the information unusable"); Neb. Rev. Stat. § 87-802 (2017) (defining the term "personal information" to exclude records where either the name or data elements are, among other things, "otherwise altered by any method or technology in such a manner that the name or data elements are unreadable"); 10 L. of P.R. § 4051 (2017) (providing safe harbor where data is not legible without the use of a special cryptographic code); Wyo. Stat. § 40-12-501(2016) (defining the term "redaction").

qualifies for notification safe harbor in any specific instance will usually require a case-specific, context-driven analysis. Moreover, it is always possible that regulators, plaintiffs, and other groups inclined to construe breach notification laws could conservatively argue that only hash functions that are sufficiently expensive, in combination with implementation of the auxiliary hashing practices discussed previously, can qualify for safe harbor.

None of the statutes discussed in this section explicitly address hashing or any of the auxiliary hashing practices, even though NIST offers detailed guidance on these issues.[54] Instead, people on both sides of the debate are left wondering what hashing practices are sufficient for hashing, for example, to render personal information inaccessible, or "unusable, unreadable, or indecipherable."

As of the time of writing, the jurisdictions that consider online account credentials to be personal information include California, Florida, Illinois, Nebraska, Nevada, Puerto Rico, Rhode Island, and Wyoming.[55] The safe harbor provisions in these statutes fall into three primary categories: (1) safe harbor applies where data is encrypted;[56] (2) safe harbor applies where the data is encrypted or protected in some alternate manner; and (3) safe harbor

---

[54] *See* Special Publication 800-63B, *supra* note 22, at 13–15.

[55] Maryland and Delaware recently passed laws updating their breach notification statutes, which, once effective, will add similar data elements to their respective definitions of personal information. *See* H.B. 974 (Md. 2017), http://mgaleg.maryland.gov/2017RS/bills/hb/hb0974E.pdf; House Substitute 1 for H.B. 180 (Del. 2017), https://legis.delaware.gov/BillDetail/26009. This article does not analyze the requirements in those bills.

[56] Some statutes also condition safe harbor on an encryption key not being compromised, but for the purposes of this article it is assumed that there has been no compromise of such keys.

applies where the data is protected using a mechanism that does not specifically refer to encryption. Within each of these categories, there are statutes that (a) provide definitions for encryption or alternate data protection mechanisms, and (b) those that do not. After examining the safe harbor provisions in these states' statutes, this article finds that hashing could, in theory, qualify for safe harbor in all eight states, but that in some of the statutes there are ambiguities or other issues that make this argument more difficult to make – most notably in Rhode Island and Nevada, and to a lesser extent in Illinois. Moreover, even where hashing can more easily qualify for safe harbor in theory, whether it qualifies in practice likely depends on the hashing algorithm used and whether any auxiliary hashing functions were used.

A. Safe Harbor Applies Where Data is Encrypted, and the Term is Defined

California: California's statute would generally consider hashing to be encryption if it rendered personal information "unusable, unreadable, or indecipherable to an unauthorized person through a security technology or methodology generally accepted in the field of information security."[57] There is little question that hashing is able to render plaintext "unusable, unreadable, or indecipherable to an unauthorized person." The next question is whether the hash functions already discussed here are "generally accepted in the field of information security." Some commentators, including a former Chief Technologist of the FTC, suggest that the inexpensive nature of SHA-1 and MD5 is not an intrinsic vulnerability in those functions. Rather,

---

[57] Cal. Civ. Code § 1798.82(i)(4).

these commentators argue that a greater number of iterations should be used to increase the preimage resistance of fast hash functions.[58] Indeed, the ability to increase the "cost," *i.e.,* the number of iterations, is a built-in feature of bcrypt that makes it particularly useful in the face of Moore's law.[59] Increasing the iterations of MD5 or SHA-1 would follow the same logic.[60] Other commentators argue that only hash functions that specifically provide resistance against GPU attacks should be used, such as bcrypt (which allegedly resists GPU attacks better due in part to its incorporation of the Blowfish block cipher). According to one well known security researcher:

> Blowfish is a block cipher with a notoriously expensive setup time. To optimize Blowfish to run much faster, you'd have to contribute a major advance to cryptography. We security practitioners are all betting people, and we usually like to place our bets on the side that demands major advances in cryptography. [The

---

[58] *See* Steven Bellovin, *Storing passwords, or the risk of a no-salt diet*, TECH@FTC BLOG (Mar. 21, 2013), https://www.ftc.gov/news-events/blogs/techftc/2013/03/storing-passwords-or-risk-no-salt-diet ("For password storage, any hash function for which one cannot compute preimages is appropriate; you just have to set the iteration count properly.").

[59] NIELS PROVOS & DAVID MAZIÈRES, *A Future-Adaptable Password Scheme*, PROCEEDINGS OF THE FREENIX TRACK: 1999 USENIX ANNUAL TECHNICAL CONFERENCE (1999), https://www.usenix.org/legacy/event/usenix99/provos/provos.pdf (last visited Jan. 23, 2018).

[60] Conversely, at least one court has refused to dismiss a claim that SHA-1 is "below the 'bare minimum' security practice" with regard to the hashing of passwords." *In Re LinkedIn User Privacy Litig.*, Case No.: 5:12-CV-03088-EJD at 15 (N.D. Cal. Mar. 28, 2014).

> creators or bcrypt also] extended Blowfish. They call theirs 'Eksblowfish.' Eksblowfish is pessimized: the setup time takes even longer than Blowfish. How long? Your call. You can make a single password trial take milliseconds, or you can make it take hours.[61]

Because of this innate resistance to GPU attacks, the argument goes that using bcrypt makes far more sense than a highly iterated MD5 or SHA-1.

NIST has also weighed in on this debate in the context of advising the federal government on its own security practices. For instance, NIST recommends the use of PBKDF2 as a key derivation function,[62] which is similar to hash function but used to derive cryptographic keys based on input passwords. Further, in its Special Publication 800-63B, *Digital Identity Guidelines Authentication and Lifecycle Management*, NIST states that "memorized secrets SHALL be salted and hashed using a suitable one-way key derivation function" and specifically lists, as examples, PBKDF2 and Balloon.[63] Moreover, as discussed further

---

[61] Thomas Ptacek, *Enough With The Rainbow Tables: What You Need To Know About Secure Password Schemes*, MATASANO SECURITY (Sep. 7, 2007), https://web.archive.org/web/20130407190430/http://chargen.matasano.com/chargen/2007/9/7/enough-with-the-rainbow-tables-what-you-need-to-know-about-s.html.

[62] NIST, Special Publication 800-132, RECOMMENDATION FOR PASSWORD-BASED KEY DERIVATION, PART 1: STORAGE APPLICATIONS at 7 (2010).

[63] Special Publication 800-63B, *supra* note 22 at 15. NIST further states that "[t]he key derivation function SHALL use an approved one-way function such as Keyed Hash Message Authentication Code (HMAC) [FIPS 198-1], any approved hash function in SP 800-107, Secure Hash Algorithm 3 (SHA-3) [FIPS 202], CMAC [SP 800-38B] or Keccak Message Authentication Code (KMAC), Customizable

below, NIST has weighed in on this topic in the context of its Federal Information Processing Standards. However, NIST's opinion does not take into consideration the existence of bcrypt.

Accordingly, while hash functions like bcrypt and PBKDF2 appear to be consensus picks as "generally accepted in the field of information technology," an argument can likely also reasonably be made that fast hash functions like MD5 and SHA-1 meet this criterion provided that an appropriate number of iterations is used to increase the preimage resistance of these hashes to GPU attacks.

Rhode Island: Rhode Island defines encryption as "the transformation of data through the use of a one hundred twenty-eight (128) bit or higher algorithmic process into a form in which there is a low probability of assigning meaning without use of a confidential process or key."[64] The reference in the statute of a requirement that the algorithm used in encryption be 128-bit or higher creates ambiguity in the context of hashing. The reference makes sense in the context of traditional encryption, where longer key lengths generally, though not always, correspond to greater difficulty in cracking ciphertext. In the context of hashing, however, it is not clear what a "128-bit or higher algorithmic process" might be. Although some types of hashing, such as the hashed message authentication code ("HMAC"), do use

---

SHAKE (cSHAKE), or ParallelHash [SP 800-185]." *Id.*
[64] R.I. Gen. L. § 11-49.3-3(2) (2017).

a key,[65] many commonly used hash functions do not.[66]

This is not to say that the statute's definition of encryption entirely precludes the application of safe harbor to hashing. One possibility is that 128-bits refers to the length of the hash itself, which is generally 128 bits or longer in the hash functions discussed in this article. It could also potentially refer to keys that are sometimes used internally by hash functions in the hashing process. However, if it is the latter, it may be difficult for some hash functions to satisfy this requirement. For instance, bcrypt, which relies on Blowfish, a symmetric key block cipher, uses keys that range between 32 and 448 bits.[67] But MD5 does not use keys at all.[68]

In light of the problematic definition of encryption in Rhode Island's data breach notification statute, it is more difficult to argue that hashed passwords qualify for safe harbor in that state. The Rhode Island legislature should strongly consider clarifying this issue, given its decision to include usernames and passwords in the definition of personal information and the reality that most entities hash

---

[65] *See* FEDERAL INFORMATION PROCESSING STANDARDS PUBLICATION 198-1, THE KEYED-HASH MESSAGE AUTHENTICATION CODE (HMAC), http://nvlpubs.nist.gov/nistpubs/FIPS/NIST.FIPS.198-1.pdf (last visited Jan. 23, 2018). According to RFC 2014, "HMAC: Keyed-Hashing for Message Authentication," keys used in HMAC should be at least as long as the byte-length of hash outputs. The byte-length for MD5 is 16, which is 128 bits. The byte output for SHA-1 is 20, or 160 bits. *See* H. KRAWCZYK et. al., HMAC: KEYED-HASHING FOR MESSAGE AUTHENTICATION (1997) https://tools.ietf.org/html/rfc2104 (last visited Jan. 23, 2018).

[66] This is true for all of the algorithms discussed in this article.

[67] *See* Bruce Schneier, *Description of a New Variable-Length Key, 64-Bit Block Cipher (Blowfish)*, in FAST SOFTWARE ENCRYPTION, CAMBRIDGE SECURITY WORKSHOP PROCEEDINGS 191(1993).

[68] *See generally* RFC 1321, https://tools.ietf.org/html/rfc1321.

passwords. However, given the legislative history discussed above, it may be that the Rhode Island legislature is not interested in broadening the definition of encryption despite the issues identified in this article.

B. *Safe Harbor Applies Where Data is Encrypted, and the Term is Not Defined*

Nevada: Nevada's statute provides safe harbor where the name and data elements are encrypted, but it does not define encryption. Notably, another, closely related Nevada statute that addresses data security does. Specifically, NRS 603A.215 defines encryption as:

> The protection of data in electronic or optical form, in storage or in transit, using... an encryption technology that has been adopted by an established standards setting body . . . which renders such data indecipherable in the absence of associated cryptographic keys necessary to enable decryption of such data.

The definition of encryption in Nevada's data security statute could be referenced by a court, plaintiff, or regulator to interpret the use of that term in the state's breach notification statute. There are, however, a number of challenges to doing so, including that (1) the Section 215 definition is not referenced in the state's breach notification statute and (2) the Section 215 definition is specifically limited to "as used in this section," i.e. Section 215. The primary argument in favor of looking to the data security statute's definition is that the two statutes are in the same chapter of the Nevada code, in close proximity to each other, and that the term is undefined in the breach notification statute.

Assuming that Section 215 would at least be considered in interpreting Nevada's beach notification statute, it is worthwhile to walk through that analysis. While Section 215's definition of encryption appears to be intended to describe encryption, not hashing, the definition could potentially apply to a hash function, primarily because hash functions generally render preimages indecipherable, albeit without a key to reverse the process. Hash functions could loosely fall under the umbrella of "encryption technology" because they are cryptographic in nature, even if hashing and encryption are technically distinguishable. At the same time, as this article makes clear, hashing is distinct from encryption, so the use of the term "encryption technology" could easily be interpreted to preclude hashing. As a result, application of the Section 215 definition could make it difficult for hashing to qualify for safe harbor.

Another question that must be answered under the Section 215 definition in the context of hashes is that the selected hash must be adopted by an established standards setting body, "including, but not limited to, the Federal Information Processing Standards issued by the National Institute of Standards and Technology."[69] The Federal Information Processing Standards, otherwise known as the FIPS, are a series of "standards and guidelines that are developed by the National Institute of Standards and Technology (NIST) for Federal computer systems" pursuant to the Information Technology Management Reform Act (Public Law 104-106).[70] Notable FIPS, for the purposes of

---

[69] Nev. Rev. Stat. Ch. 603A.215(5)(b).
[70] NIST, FIPS GENERAL INFORMATION, https://www.nist.gov/information-technology-laboratory/fips-general-information (last visited Jan. 23, 2018).

this article, are 140-2, *Security Requirements for Cryptographic Modules*, FIPS 180-4, *Secure Hash Standard (SHS)*, and FIPS 202, *SHA-3 Standard: Permutation-Based Hash and Extendable-Output Functions*. NIST has also issued special publications in which they endorse specific hashing algorithms, including Special Publication 800-132, *Recommendation for Password-Based Key Derivation, Part 1: Storage Application*, and Special Publication 800-63B, *Digital Identity Guidelines Authentication and Lifecycle Management*. Other standards setting bodies have likewise endorsed specific hash functions.

If the Section 215 definition is not applied to the undefined term "encryption," it is unclear whether hashed passwords would qualify for safe harbor in Nevada. Because the term is undefined and preexisted the addition of user credentials to the definition of personal information, it is possible to argue that the Nevada legislature overlooked this issue while intending for industry-standard security protections for passwords to be subject to safe harbor. At the same time, one could also easily argue that the term "encryption," by definition, precludes hashing from qualifying for safe harbor. This is an issue that the Nevada legislature should consider addressing as soon as possible.

C. Safe Harbor Applies Where the Data is Encrypted or Protected in Some Alternate Manner, and the Terms are Defined

Nebraska: Nebraska's statute provides safe harbor if either the name or the data elements are "encrypted, redacted, or otherwise altered by any method or technology in such a manner that the name or data elements are unreadable."[71] Although the statute defines both "encrypted" and "redacted," it is not necessary to analyze whether hashing would satisfy those definitions, as it also carves out from the definition of personal information records where "either the name or the data elements are . . . otherwise altered by any method or technology in such a manner that the name or data elements are unreadable."[72] Hashing would reasonably satisfy this requirement. The only question in this context would be whether a hash that would be trivial to crack would reasonably be considered "unreadable."

D. Safe Harbor Applies Where the Data is Encrypted or Protected in Some Alternate Manner, and the Terms are Not Defined

Florida: Florida's statute provides notification safe harbor for data that is "encrypted, secured or modified by any other method or technology that removes elements that personally identify an individual or that otherwise renders the information unusable."[73] Hashing generally qualifies for this exception. Hash functions that create hashes from passwords arguably render the information unusable. However, whether the data is truly unusable or rather can realistically be cracked likely hinges on the hash function used and whether the auxiliary hashing practices have been implemented, as previously discussed.

Illinois: The Illinois statute provides safe harbor for data that is encrypted or redacted, but it does not define

---

[71] Neb. Rev. Stat. § 87-802(5)(a).
[72] *Id.*
[73] Fla. Stat. § 501.171(g)(2).

either term.[74] Despite the lack of definitions, it is possible that hashing a password could meet the intent of the law, particularly as the safe harbor provision is included specifically in the portion of the definition of personal information that includes user credentials.[75] The same challenges discussed in the context of the Nevada statute would apply to the undefined use of the term "encryption" in the Illinois statute. However, it is easier to argue that hashing qualifies for safe harbor in Illinois in light of the statute's undefined use of the term "redacted." Nonetheless, this is an issue that the Illinois legislature should consider addressing as soon as possible.

E. *Safe Harbor Applies Where the Data is Protected Using a Mechanism that Does Not Specifically Refer to Encryption, and the Terms are Defined*

Wyoming: Wyoming's statute provides safe harbor where the data elements are "redacted," which is defined as "alteration or truncation of data such that no more than five (5) digits of the data elements . . . are accessible as part of the personal information."[76] Hash functions could potentially fall under this definition. Hash functions alter data such that no digits – let alone five – of the data elements are readable or otherwise usable. At the same time, the use of the term "digits" is ambiguous in this context because a

---

[74] *See* 815 Ill. Comp. Stat. § 530/5 (2017).
[75] This language was added at the same time user credentials were added to the definition of personal information, which may indicate legislative intent for hashing to qualify for safe harbor. *See* HB1260 (Ill. 2016), http://www.ilga.gov/legislation/publicacts/99/PDF/099-0503.pdf.
[76] Wyo. Stat. § 40-12-501(a)(8).

password may consist only of letters and special characters and contain no digits at all. Assuming the term does apply to alphanumeric values, the primary question under this statute would be whether the underlying passwords are "accessible" even though hashed, which in turn likely hinges on the hash function used and whether the auxiliary hashing practices have been implemented, as previously discussed.

It is also worth noting that due to a quirk in the statute, it is not clear if the Wyoming statute provides any safe harbor at all for "redacted" data. This is because the definition of "redact" appears to apply only to "the data elements provided in subparagraphs (vii)(A) through (D) of this subsection," all of which were repealed in 2015. Thus, the definition technically does not apply to the statute as drafted today. This is an issue the Wyoming legislature should address as quickly as possible.

F. Safe Harbor Applies Where the Data is Protected Using a Mechanism that Does Not Specifically Refer to Encryption, and the Terms are Not Defined

Puerto Rico: Puerto Rico's statute requires notification if personal information is "legible enough so that in order to process it there is no need to use a *special cryptographic code*."[77] The term "special cryptographic code" is not defined. Despite the lack of a definition, it seems likely that hashing a password would meet the intent of the law. Hash functions are cryptographic in nature and create an output that is theoretically not usable or readable even when an attacker has possession of the hash, just as with ciphertext. Of course, as discussed previously, it is possible

---

[77] 10 L. P.R. Ann. § 4051(a).

that a fast hash in combination with a weak password might not be considered to qualify by some judges, regulators, or plaintiffs. Thus, the use of an expensive hash function in combination with the implementation of the auxiliary hashing practices remains an important consideration.

VI.   CONCLUSION

As is evident from the above overview, not all hashes are created equal. The "expensiveness" of the function, the presence of a salt (and sometimes a pepper), the function's resistance to GPU attacks, and the organization's password policies, among other things, constitute criteria that must be assessed when determining if a particular use of a password hash function is sufficiently secure to qualify for safe harbor. Legislators in states that consider usernames and passwords to constitute personal information, or that are considering amending their statutes to do so, should recognize that the vast majority of organizations protect that information through hashing. Accordingly, they should make clear in their states' breach notification statutes that hashing can qualify for breach notification safe harbor as a general matter. Doing so does not require making explicit reference to hashing, provided that the language used, either in a separate definition or in the definition of "personal information," clearly applies to hashing. A definition that would meet this criterion, for example, would provide safe harbor where data elements are "encrypted, redacted, or altered in a manner that renders the elements unusable, unreadable, or indecipherable to an unauthorized person."

Legislators also need to take into consideration that some hashes would not be secure enough to warrant safe harbor. They must therefore consider how best to identify in their states' statutes the minimum acceptable qualifying criteria for the expensiveness of the hash function, the type of salt and/or pepper, and the auxiliary hashing practices that must also be implemented alongside the selected hash function, out of recognition that notification should not be necessary when passwords are hashed in a sufficiently secure manner.   Aside from listing these criteria individually, a statute could potentially include, among other options, (1) a requirement that if a hashing function is used on passwords, the function and password policy used be configured consistent with the Memorized Secret Verifiers section of NIST's Special Publication 800-63B, *Digital Identity Guidelines Authentication and Lifecycle Management*; and/or (2) an option to have an expert certify that a specialized password cracking rig would be unable to crack more than a specific (minute) percentage of the password hashes stored in a table in the event of a breach.

"Playing With Fire" An Inter-Agency Working Group Proposal for Connected Vehicle Technology and the DSRC Mandate

Christopher Kolezynski[*]

INTRODUCTION

The windshield wipers ran and the radio blared as Ben Makuch frantically and unsuccessfully tried to turn down the music. Things would only get worse. Soon, Ben Makuch lost control of the steering, braking, and eventually the transmission while driving a 2014 Jeep Cherokee. Security researchers, Chris Valasek and former NSA hacker, Dr. Charlie Miller engineered the hack. During the interview, Makuch asked Miller "Is there ever a scenario where you think a hacker could get access to a vulnerability in a car…just like this…[causing] a million cars t[o] just turn off? To which Miller shrugged and nonchalantly responded, "I could of done that….I could have made all the transmissions go to neutral for a million cars."[1]

[*] *Christopher Kolezynski, J.D.* from the Cleveland-Marshall College of Law, May 2018; B.A., Cleveland State University, 2014. Special to thanks to my mother, Marcia Kolezynski, my father, Gary Kolezynski, my sister, Jennifer Kolezynski, and my great aunt Eileen May, for their unconditional support. Further thanks to dear friend, Stephen Vano, who inspired the path I have chosen.
[1] *CYBERWAR: The Zero Day Market*, (Vice Productions Inc. 2016) (Miller was never paid for his work. Although one year later Chrysler changed policy and began a company bounty program paying researchers who found vulnerabilities in their cars. They were the first major American car company to do so).

Miller reported this vulnerability to Chrysler who took 9 months to work on the problem before Miller, in fear for the safety of millions, decided to go public. Chrysler fixed the vulnerability one week later.[2] There are two important lessons to learn from this story: (1) connected vehicles will materially increase the level of risk on the roads; (2) and some companies may not promptly address these risks.

The vulnerability exposed by Miller would have allowed the remote disabling of millions of transmissions because of the Uconnect head unit, a connected vehicle technology, connecting Jeep Cherokees and other vehicles. These head units are installed in Chrysler, Dodge, Jeep, Fiat, and Ram vehicles and provide features such as remote engine start and vehicle unlock from the user's phone as well as in car streaming services, GPS navigation and app sharing. The two security researchers who conducted the study also concluded "the[ir] attack on the entertainment system seem[ed] to work on any Chrysler vehicle with Uconnect from late 2013, all of 2014, and early 2015. [Although] [t]hey've only tested their full set of physical hacks...on a Jeep Cherokee...they believe...most of their attacks could be tweaked to work on any Chrysler vehicle with the vulnerable Uconnect head unit."[3] Jeep and Chrysler are not alone. Some of the most popular vehicles on the road, such as the Toyota Prius and 2014 Ford Fusion, could also

---

[2] *Id.* (Miller explains "car companies are so new to this. Most car companies, you don't even know who you would contact to tell them you found a vulnerability.").

[3] Andy Greenberg, *Hackers Remotely Kill a Jeep on the Highway With Me In It*, WIRED (July 7, 2015), https://www.wired.com/2015/07/hackers-remotely-kill-jeep-highway/ (last visited Jan 31, 2018).

be subject to these types of hacks.[4] Other hacks have taken advantage of popular connected vehicle technologies, such as Onstar. The Onstar hack allowed remote disabling of the brakes among other attacks and took 5 years to fix.[5] Other

---

[4] Victoria Woollaston, *The 20 Most Hackable CARS Revealed: Report Lists the Smart Vehicles That Are Most at Risk of Having Their Systems Hijacked*, DAILY MAIL (August 8, 2016), http://www.dailymail.co.uk/sciencetech/article-2719866/The-20-hackable-CARS-revealed-Report-lists-smart-vehicles-risk-having-systems-hijacked.html#ixzz4LNTrEGFG (last visited Jan 31, 2018) (*citing*, Charlie Miller & Chris Valasek, *A Survey of Remote Automotive Attack Surfaces*, Black Hat Security Conference in Las Vegas 2014) (These vehicles include; the Cadillac Escalade, Ford Fusion, Dodge Ram 3500, BMW X3, Chrysler 300, Range Rover Evoque, Toyota Prius, Toyota Prius, Infiniti Q50, Audi A8, Infiniti G37, BMW3 Series, BMW i12Dodge Viper, and the Honda Accord LX.In 2013, Chris Valasek and Charlie Miller hacked a 2010 Toyota Prius and changed speedometer readings resulting in triggering of the cars collision protection features, disabled braking, and controlled the horn on the vehicle.). *See* also Babb, P., *Video: Watch what happens when a Prius gets hacked*, InfoWorld (Aug. 7, 2013), https://www.infoworld.com/article/2611599/hacking/video--watch-what-happens-when-a-prius-gets-hacked.html (last visited Jan 31, 2018). *See also* Jonathan Vanian, *Security Experts Hack Cars*, Fortune (January 26, 2016), http://fortune.com/2016/01/26/security-experts-hack-cars/ (last visited Jan 31, 2018)*See also* Rob Crilly, *Thousands of cars vulnerable to keyless theft, according to researchers*, The Telegraph (August 8, 2015) https://www.telegraph.co.uk/news/uknews/11808814/Thousands-of-cars-vulnerable-to-keyless-theft-according-to-researchers.html (last visited Feb 4, 2018) (The following vehicles have had their keyless entry hacked allowing for easy theft of the vehicle without enabling the alarm. Audi A3, A4, and A6, BMW 730d, Citreon DS4 Crossback, Ford Galaxy, Ford Eco-Sport, Honda HR-V, Hyundai Santa Fe, Kia Optima, Lexus RX 450, Range Rover Evoque, Renault Traffic, Mazda CX-5, MINI Clubman, Mitsubishi Outlander, Nissan Qashqai +2, Nissan Leaf, Opel Ampera, SsangYong Tivoli XDi, Subaru Levorg, Toyota RAV 4, VW Golf 7 GTD, VW Touran 5T.)
[5] A. Greenberg, *GM Took 5 Years to Fix a Full-Takeover Hack in*

cars that have been hacked include the Mitsubishi Outlander Hybrid,[6] Tesla Model S,[7] and the 2009 Chevy Impala, which was the test vehicle for the Onstar hack.[8]

Millions of Onstar Cars, WIRED (September 10, 2015), https://www.wired.com/2015/09/gm-took-5-years-fix-full-takeover-hack-millions-onstar-cars (last visited Jan 31, 2018).

[6] Nellie Bowels, *Yet another car can be hacked – this time it's the Mitsubishi Outlander Hybrid*, THE GUARDIAN (June 26, 2016), https://www.theguardian.com/technology/2016/jun/06/mitsubishi-outlander-car-hacked-security (last visited Jan 31, 2018).

[7] Andrea Peterson, *Researchers Remotely Hack Tesla Model S*, THE WASHINGTON POST (September 20, 2016), https://www.washingtonpost.com/news/the-switch/wp/2016/09/20/researchers-remotely-hack-tesla-model-s (last visited Jan 31, 2018).

[8] Bowels, *supra* note 6 (It took 5 years for GM to fix this particular vulnerability!); *See also* Giles, M., *Thanks To This Device, Stealing Your Car Has Never Been Easier*, POPULAR SCIENCE (August 6, 2015), http://www.popsci.com/thanks-device-stealing-your-car-has-never-been-easier?con=TrueAnthem&dom=fb&src=SOC&utm_campaign=&utm_content=588e19b8f6d7a10006969bd2&utm_medium=&utm_source (last visited Jan 31, 2018).

> "Samy Kamkar is a car buff. The cyber security expert enjoys tinkering, particularly in the intersection of automation and the Internet of Things. "I love the new technology that car companies are introducing," he says, "but I worry whether the manufacturers are actually paying attention to the security of these connected vehicles." That's why, last week, he unveiled a recent four-wheel hack of a friend's Chevy Volt, cracking the OnStar, which is owned by General Motors, through a device he built called OwnStar."
> *Id.*

The advancement of connected vehicle technology brings with it new risks. One potentially catastrophic risk would be for millions of cars to be remotely hijacked, leading to a disaster approaching the scale of the September 11 attacks.[9] While such a scenario is hopefully remote, it remains a possibility because of a proposed mandate of Vehicle-to-Vehicle technology by the National Highway Traffic and Safety Administration ("NHTSA").[10] NHTSA proposed in 2014 to mandate the use of Dedicated Short Range Communication ("DSRC") devices in all new light vehicles.[11]

These DSRC devices are a connected vehicle technology, utilizing the 5.9 GHz bandwidth, allowing vehicles to transmit Basic Safety Messages between each other. This information includes messaging about road conditions and nearby vehicles. Never before have vehicles been connected on such a wide scale.

"[T]he one thing that has prevented cyberterrorists from…infecting thousands of cars with malware designed to crash them…has been the inability of cars to communicate with each other…You can do it on a one-car basis. You can't yet do it on a 100,000-car basis."[12] On March 17, 2016, the

---

[9] Kohler & Colbert-Taylor, *Current Law and Potential Legal Issues Pertaining to Automated, Autonomous and Connected Vehicles*, 31 Santa Clara High Tech. L.J. 99, 133 (2015).

[10] Federal Motor Vehicle Safety Standards: Vehicle-to-Vehicle (V2V) Communications, 79 Fed. Reg. 161 (proposed Aug. 20,2014) (to be codified at 49 C.F.R. pt. 571).

[11] *Id.*; *See also* Federal Motor Vehicle Safety Standards: Vehicle-to-Vehicle (V2V) Communications, 82 Fed. Reg., 3860 (proposed Jan. 12, 2017) (explaining, "[l]ight vehicles include passenger cars, vans, minivans, sport utility vehicles, crossover utility vehicles and light pickup trucks with a gross vehicle weight rating less than or equal to 10,000 pounds.").

[12] Open Technology Institute & Public Knowledge, *Petition for*

Federal Bureau of Investigation ("FBI") released a public announcement warning "the general public and manufacturers...to maintain awareness of...cybersecurity threats related to connected vehicle technologies[13] The FBI explained, "[m]odern motor vehicles often include new connected vehicle technologies that aim to provide...added safety features...[and] [a]ftermarket devices are also providing consumers with new features to monitor the status of their vehicles....[However, because of] this increased connectivity, it is important that consumers and manufacturers maintain awareness of potential cyber security threats."[14] In an example case discussed in the announcement, NHTSA had to recall over one million vehicles as a result of the discovery of multiple remote exploits.[15]

As an effect of the DSRC mandate, the Federal Communications Commission ("FCC") was petitioned to issue a stay on operation of the connected vehicle technology. The requested emergency stay would work by not allowing operation of DSRC devices in the 5.9ghz bandwidth, which falls under FCC jurisdiction.[16] The petition explains, "[t]he DSRC service lacks rules to protect

---

Rulemaking and Request for Emergency Stay of Operation of Dedicated Short-Range Communications Service in the 5.850-5.9925 GHZ Band (5.9 GHZ Band), iv-v (June 28, 2016).

[13] FBI, *Public Service Announcement: Motor Vehicles Increasingly Vulnerable to Remote Exploits,* (March 17, 2016), https://www.ic3.gov/media/2016/160317.aspx (last visited Jan 31, 2018).

[14] *Id.*

[15] *Id.*

[16] Open Technology Institute & Public Knowledge, *Petition for Rulemaking and Request for Emergency Stay of Operation of Dedicated Short-Range Communications Service in the 5.850-5.9925 GHZ Band (5.9 GHZ Band)* (June 28, 2016).

user privacy or to protect DSRC units from malware or other forms of cybersecurity attacks." The FCC took notice of this petition and opened the issue for public comment on July 25, 2016.[17]

The problem this inevitably creates is one of agency jurisdiction. NHTSA asserted in their 2014 Advanced Notice of Proposed Rulemaking that "the agency was confident its existing legal authority would cover [V2V Technologies]."[18] However, the FCC has jurisdiction over "wire and radio,"[19] specifically the 5.9 GHz band utilized by DSRC devices. Even more complicating, the Federal Trade Commission has jurisdiction over "unfair and deceptive trade practices [including data security] in or affecting commerce"[20] and NHTSA has jurisdiction over the motor vehicle equipment[21] that creates this data. Therefore, the vehicles themselves, their component technologies, and the data they create could be subject to FTC, FCC, and NHTSA regulations.

This evolving presence of connected vehicle technology will inevitably lead to potential jurisdictional hurdles, duplicative, potentially inconsistent regulations, and endangered consumers. As more capabilities, connectivity, and features are added the attack surface will widen[22] and the amount of vulnerabilities will increase. On

---

[17] Lydia Beyoud, *FCC Studying Cybersecurity of Connected Vehicle Tech*, BLOOMBERG BNA (July 27, 2016), http://www.bna.com/fcc-studying-cybersecurity-n73014445537 (last visited Jan 31, 2018).
[18] Federal Motor Vehicle Safety Standards: Vehicle-to-Vehicle (V2V) Communications, 79 Fed. Reg. 161 (proposed Aug. 20,2014) (to be codified at 49 C.F.R. pt. 571).
[19] 47 U.S.C. § 151 (2017).
[20] 15 U.S.C § 45(a) (2012).
[21] 49 U.S.C. § 30101 (2013).
[22] Greg Rogers, *NHTSA's Proposed Rule Requires Cars to Talk to Each Other*, Eno Transportation Weekly (Dec. 16, 2016),

the bright side, connected vehicle technologies, specifically the current DSRC mandate, presents an opportunity to promote a collaborative regulatory approach through an inter-agency working group.

The remainder of this article will be divided into four (4) parts. First, the history of DSRC rulemaking, including discussion of the security and privacy risks associated with connected vehicle technology, and the security and privacy risks specific to the current Notice of Proposed Rulemaking will be explored. Second, I will propose an Inter-Agency Working Group composed of the FCC, FTC, and NHTSA to build upon the current rulemaking. In doing so, I will explore the history of Inter-Agency Working Groups in relation to emerging technologies, the benefits of joint policymaking and explain the benefits of involving FTC and FCC expertise in the rulemaking process. Third, I will review agency jurisdiction and review how it applies to DSRC. Finally, I will conclude the best approach to the problem is the development of an Inter-Agency Working Group, including the FTC, FCC, and NHTSA because as it stands, vehicles equipped under current DSRC rules, would simply be *"Unsafe at Any Speed."*[23]

---

https://www.enotrans.org/article/nhtsas-proposed-rule-requires-cars-talk (last visited Jan 31, 2018) (explaining "[f]or each node that is added to a network, there is a new set of vulnerabilities. Deploying hundreds of thousands, and eventually millions, of vehicles that are connected to a single communications network creates a slew of vulnerabilities.").

[23] RALPH NADER, UNSAFE AT ANY SPEED: THE DESIGNED-IN DANGERS OF THE AMERICAN AUTOMOBILE, (1965).

I.   DSRC RULEMAKING: SECURITY AND PRIVACY RISKS

   A. History

        In August 2014, NHTSA issued an Advanced Notice
of Proposed Rulemaking for mandating DSRC devices in all
new light cars.[24] After collecting 926 comments, some of
which focused on the danger of such a network being
hacked,[25] NHTSA submitted a Notice for Proposed
Rulemaking to the Office of Management and Budget in
January 2016.[26] The Notice for Proposed Rulemaking was
issued in December 2016.[27] The summary explains, "This
rulemaking would require that all light vehicles be capable
of V2V communication by use of on-board dedicated short-
range radio communication (DSRC) devices, which would
broadcast messages about a vehicle's speed, heading, brake
status, and other information to other vehicles and receive
the same information from the messages with extended
range and 'line-of-sight' capabilities."[28] NHTSA explained
in a Press Release following the Notice of the Proposed Rule
that the goal of the technology is to prevent "hundreds of
thousands of crashes."[29] In support of this claim, NHTSA

---

[24] Federal Motor Vehicle Safety Standards: Vehicle-to-Vehicle (V2V)
Communications, 79 Fed. Reg. 161 (proposed Aug. 20, 2014) (to be
codified at 49 C.F.R. pt. 571).
[25] *Id.* at https://www.regulations.gov/document?D=NHTSA-2014-
0022-0002.
[26] Federal Motor Vehicle Safety Standards 150 - Vehicle-to-Vehicle
(V2V) Communication, 79 Fed. Reg. 161 (proposed January 12, 2016)
(to be codified at 49 C.F.R. 571.150).
[27] Federal Motor Vehicle Safety Standards; V2V Communications, 49
CFR Part 571 (proposed Dec. 13 2016) (to be codified at 49 CFR pt.
571).
[28] *Id.* at https://www.regulations.gov/docket?D=NHTSA-2016-0126.
[29] *U.S. DOT advances deployment of Connected Vehicle Technology to*

states that "V2V communications can detect developing threat situations hundreds of yards away, and often in situations in which the driver and on-board sensors alone cannot detect the threat."[30] The technology works by "requiring V2V devices to "speak the same language" through standardized messaging."[31] The most recent Notice of Proposed Rulemaking has received 463 comments and the public comment period ends on April 12, 2017.[32]

The cybersecurity concerns about implementing this technology can be categorized into two broad categories: security and privacy.

B.   Security Risks and Increasing the Attack Surface

Security concerns arise from the technologies used to connect vehicles. For example, one report from a leading security company suggests there may be fourteen (14) different ways a hacker could gain access to a car's operating system alone.[33] Other possibilities exist too, as one

---

prevent hundreds of thousands of crashes, (2016), https://www.nhtsa.gov/press-releases/us-dot-advances-deployment-connected-vehicle-technology-prevent-hundreds-thousands (last visited Dec. 28, 2017).

[30] *Id.*

[31] *Id.*

[32] Federal Motor Vehicle Safety Standards: Vehicle-to-Vehicle (V2V) Communications, 82 Fed. Reg. 3854 (proposed Jan. 12, 2017), available at https://www.regulations.gov/docket?D=NHTSA-2016-0126.

[33] Open Technology Institute & Public Knowledge, *Petition for Rulemaking and Request for Emergency Stay of Operation of Dedicated Short-Range Communications Service in the 5.850-5.9925 GHZ Band (5.9 GHZ Band)*, iv (June 28, 2016) (*citing*, Intel, *Automotive Security Best Practices: Recommendations for security and privacy in the era of the next generation car (2015)* ("Intel Whitepaper"), available at

overarching concern of any new technology is its expansion of the attack surface, which, in the case of connected cars, would be significant in light of the component technologies involved.

The FBI and DOT acknowledged this possibility noting in a Public Service Announcement that cars are becoming increasingly more vulnerable through "remote exploits."[34] Despite these warnings, NHTSA continues to push DSRC technology forward.[35] The State Department of Transportation of California ("CALTRANS") identified one such example: "the DSRC system is designed to use predetermined message structures to identify current highway and vehicle conditions. These message structures do not include the ability to install malware … from one car to another."[36]

---

http://www.intel.com/content/www/us/en/automotive/automotive-security-best-practices-white-paper.html (last visited Jan 31, 2018).

[34] *Id.*; *See also* Senator Ed Markey, *Tracking & Hacking: Security and Privacy Risks Put American Drivers at Risk*,(Feb. 2015), available at http://www.markey.senate.gov/imo/media/doc/2015-02-06_MarkeyReport- Tracking_Hacking_CarSecurity%202.pdf. (The 2015 Markey Report found that "[m]ost automobile manufacturers were unaware of or unable to report on past hacking incidents. Security measures to prevent remote access to vehicle electronics [wer]e inconsistent and haphazard across all auto manufacturers…[and] [o]nly two automobile manufacturers were able to describe any capabilities to diagnose or meaningfully respond to an infiltration in real-time, and most say they rely on technologies that cannot be used for this purpose at all.").

[35] Senator Ed Markey, *Tracking & Hacking: Security and Privacy Risks Put American Drivers at Risk* (Feb. 2015), http://www.markey.senate.gov/imo/media/doc/2015-02-06_MarkeyReport- Tracking_Hacking_CarSecurity%202.pdf. (last visited Jan 31, 2018).

[36] Comments of the State of California Department of Transportation, *In the Matter of Open Technology Institute & Public Knowledge,*

Malware is data or computer code just like any other software. It does not identify itself as malware, unless assigned a signature by antivirus companies or is otherwise detectable, and is often injected into pdf or word documents as seen in phishing attacks via email. Furthermore, much malware is designed to be covert. This can be done through encryption and other methodologies. Zero-day exploits are by definition undetectable because no one is aware that the vulnerabilities they exploit even exist.[37] Some of the covert qualities found in worms, a type of malware, include polymorphic or metamorphic features.[38] Every new copy made of a polymorphic worm, is done so using slightly modified code. Metamorphic worms can rewrite their own code and change their behavior. Both of these serve to hide detection.[39]

Certainly, one could design malware to emulate the predetermined message structures used to communicate with other vehicles. Furthermore, radio, specifically the 900 MHz band, has already been used to transmit data while the adversary remains nearly undetectable.[40] One example specific to DSRC is the delay of Basic Safety Messages caused by harmful interference. The Alliance of Automobile Manufacturers   and   Association   of   Automobile

---

Petition for Rulemaking and Request for Emergency Stay of Operation of Dedicated Short-Range Communications Service in the 5.850-5.9925 GHZ Band (5.9 GHZ Band), 9 (August 19, 2016).

[37] WILLAM STALLINGS & LAWRIE BROWN, COMPUTER SECURITY PRINCIPLES AND PRACTICE, 216 (3d. 2015).

[38] *Id.*

[39] *Id.*

[40] Lucia Constantin, *Hackers show off long-distance Wi-Fi radio proxy at DEF CON*, PC WORLD (August 10, 2015), http://www.pcworld.com/article/2968232/security/hackers-show-off-longdistance-wifi-radio-proxy-at-def-con.html (last visited Jan 31, 2018).

Manufacturers wrote to the FCC in 2013 about their concerns regarding harmful interference caused by U-NII-3 and U-NII-4 devices.[41] When one company was asked about cybersecurity protections for DSRC units, they responded "[w]hat's being exchanged between vehicles is just data . . . There's no possibility of a virus being spread between cars.'" However, all information exchanged through a computer network is ""just data" – viruses included….[and] [c]ybercriminals and terrorists…will use this attack vector…exchanging "just data" to potentially devastating effect."[42] The United States Government Accountability Office ("GAO") report on Vehicle-to-Vehicle technologies states that "[o]f the 21 experts…interviewed, 12 cited the technical development of a V2V communication security system as a great or very great challenge to the deployment of V2V technologies."[43]

Moreover, due to the projected growth of connectivity among cars, there is a strong likelihood attackers will focus on obtaining financial gain through hacking vehicles. This may be achieved in several different ways: remote unlocking and theft of vehicles, ransoming control of the vehicle until receipt of payment through untraceable bitcoin, accessing data located on driver's cell

---

[41] The Alliance of Automobile Manufacturers and Association of Automobile Manufacturers *5.9 GHz DSRC Connected Vehicles for Intelligent Transportation Systems*, (Sep. 13, 2013) https://ecfsapi.fcc.gov/file/7520943378.pdf.

[42] Comments of Public Knowledge et al., *In the matter of Petition for Rulemaking and Request for Emergency Stay of Operation of Dedicated Short-Range Communications Service in the 5.850-5.9925 GHZ Band (5.9 GHZ Band)*, 3 (August 24, 2016).

[43] US Gov't Accountability Off., Intelligent Transportation Systems: Vehicle to Vehicle Technologies Offer Safety Benefits but a Variety of Deployment Challenges Exist GAO-14-13, at 21 (2013).

phones through USB ports in the vehicle, or listening to conversations inside a vehicle via Bluetooth connectivity.[44]

C. Privacy Risks

Privacy concerns are raised by the transmission of data between cars, the type of data gathered, where that data is stored, and how it is used. In order to protect data in transmission, especially personal identification information, data will "need to be robustly anonymized, strongly encrypted, and securely protected to avoid being vulnerable."[45] Auto manufacturers who sell their vehicles in other countries, such as Europe, may have to meet even more stringent standards regarding the data created by connected vehicle technology. One threat presented by connected vehicle data is that "information...can be correlated with other information...., including the location where the vehicle is regularly parked overnight, ... to profile the likely user...and to predict the user's actions."[46]

The Markey Report, published by Senator Edward Markey in 2015, was developed by surveying 16 major automobile manufacturers regarding the cybersecurity and privacy protections of connected vehicle technologies. The Report found that the majority of auto manufacturers offered technology features that gathered and sent data to a data center, sometimes run by a third party.[47] Most of these

---

[44] Burke Katie, *What do car hackers really want? Security threats are mostly about money*, AUTOMOTIVENEWS (October17,2016) http://www.autonews.com/article/20161017/OEM06/310179880/what-do-car-hackers-really-want (last visited Jan 31, 2018).

[45] Dorothy J. Glancy, *Privacy in Autonomous Vehicles*, 52 Santa Clara L. Rev. 1171, 1205 (2012).

[46] *Id.* at 1196.

[47] Markey, *supra*, *Tracking & Hacking: Security and Privacy Risks Put*

manufacturers could not describe measures that were in place to protect the data, although many utilized the data in a variety of ways.[48] Furthermore, "[c]ustomers [we]re often not explicitly made aware of data collection and, when they [we]re, they often cannot opt out without disabling valuable features, such as navigation."[49] Such poor data protection practices have already resulted in telecommunications companies being fined millions of dollars by the FCC.[50] One independent commentator has called for the NHTSA to conduct a more comprehensive analysis of these privacy concerns to ensure personally identifiable information is not collected without proper consent."[51]

American Drivers at Risk, (Feb 2015), https://www.markey.senate.gov/imo/media/doc/2015-02-06_MarkeyReport-Tracking_Hacking_CarSecurity%202.pdf (last visited Jan 31, 2018).

[48] *Id.*

[49] *Id.* (The SPY Car Act explicitly addresses the concern over loss of navigation features when opting out of data collection); *See supra* note 32.

[50] ENFORCEMENT BUREAU, *FCC Plans $10M Fine For Carriers That Breached Consumer Privacy*, FCC (Oct. 24, 2014), https://www.fcc.gov/document/fcc-plans-10m-fine-carriers-breached-consumer-privacy. *See also* Daniel J Solove & Paul M. Schwartz, *Privacy Law Fundamentals*, IAPP 2 (2011); Max Green, *15 of the biggest data breach settlements and HIPAA fines*, Becker's Health IT & CIO REVIEW (October 14, 2015), http://www.beckershospitalreview.com/healthcare-information-technology/15-of-the-biggest-data-breach-settlements-hipaa-fines.html; Aruna Viswanatha, *Morgan Stanley Fined 1 Million for Client Data Breach*, THE WALL ST. JOURNAL (June 8, 2016) (As the above articles illustrate, failure to account for attacks and subsequent data breaches could just as easily lead to massive liability for auto companies through privacy based tort actions or general negligence), http://www.wsj.com/articles/morgan-stanley-fined-1-million-for-client-data-breach-1465415374.

[51] Comments of the Electronic Privacy Information Center, Federal

As a result of the growing concern for privacy issues related to vehicle created data, other efforts to protect the public have also been proposed. Senators Ed Markey and Richard Blumenthal introduced the Security and Privacy in Your Car Act ("SPY Car Act") to the Senate on July 21, 2015. The SPY Car Act would require the NHTSA to issue regulations that would require vehicles with accessible data or control signals to be capable of detecting, reporting, and stopping attempts to intercept such driving data or [attempt to] control the vehicle."[52] Further, The SPY Car Act would require the Federal Trade Commission to: "(1) require motor vehicles to notify owners or lessees about the collection, transmission, retention, and use of driving data; (2) provide owners or lessees with the option to terminate such data collection and retention...without losing navigation tools...and (3) prohibit manufacturers from using collected information for advertising or marketing purposes without the owner's or lessee's consent." The SPY Car Act takes note of not only security concerns but also addresses concerns over consumer privacy.

Motor Vehicle Safety Standards: Vehicle-to-Vehicle (V2V) Communications, 79 Fed. Reg. 161 (comment sent October 20, 2014) (to be codified at 49. C.F.R. 571) ("NHTSA should complete a more detailed privacy and security assessment of V2V communications. Additionally, NHTSA should: (1) not collect PII without the express, written authorization of the vehicle owner; (2) ensure that no data will be stored either locally or remotely; (3) require end-to-end encryption of V2V communications, including the basic safety messages ("BSMs"); (4) require end-to-end anonymity; and (5) require auto manufacturers to adhere to the Consumer Privacy Bill of Rights.").
[52] Security and Privacy in Your Car Act, S. 1806, 114th Cong. (2015).

D. V2V NPRM Security Measures and Concerns

The messaging employed in NHTSA's proposed mandate would have a range around 300 meters.[53] The NPRM proposes to mandate DSRC technology during the manufacturing stage, but also leaves open the possibility of aftermarket installations or the use of handheld devices. The NPRM explains that having these options is integral to reaching "optimal safety benefits of a [vehicle to vehicle] cooperative safety network."[54] However, the inclusion of aftermarket products or handheld devices could introduce additional vulnerabilities.[55] Furthermore, the NPRM refers to two possible future applications of the vehicle to vehicle ("V2V") communication system: "Intersection Movement Assist [and] Left Turn Assist."[56] While both of these

---

[53] Cahill, Kohler & Laurenza, *NHTSA Issues Proposed V2V Crash Avoidance Technology Rule*, LEXOLOGY (Dec. 19,2016), available at http://www.lexology.com/library/detail.aspx?g=22cdefa8-99f2-4dd7-bcc2-caabd953346c.

[54] *Id.*

[55] NHTSA, Vehicle-to-Vehicle Communications: Readiness of V2V Technology for
Application, DOT HS 81214, 29 (August 2014), available at https://www.nhtsa.gov/sites/nhtsa.dot.gov/files/readiness-of-v2v-technology-for-application-812014.pdf. ("An aftermarket V2V communication device provides advisories and warnings to the driver of a vehicle similar to those provided by an OEM installed V2V device. These devices, however, may not be as fully integrated into the vehicle as an OEM device...For example, a "self-contained" V2V aftermarket safety device could only connect to a power source, and otherwise would operate independently...Aftermarket V2V devices can be added to a vehicle at a vehicle dealership, as well as by authorized dealers or installers of automotive equipment. Some aftermarket V2V devices (e.g., cell phones with apps) are portable and can be standalone units carried by the operator, the passenger, or pedestrians.").

[56] *Id.*

functions are still limited to providing warnings, there incorporation shows NHTSA's intention of providing for different and additional types of warnings as the V2V communication system progresses. The NPRM notes that V2V and Vehicle to Infrastructure communications are "warnings-only systems."[57] Yet, physical control of a vehicle might be possible if the attacker merely uses V2V to access other onboard computer systems such as the Uconnect head unit exploited by Charlie Miller or the vehicles electronic control unit.[58] For example, if V2V was used as a pathway to access the electronic control unit this might result in the ability to disable braking or the exploitation of other features employed by that electronic control unit. Although this is seemingly more frightening and equally difficult, the danger of vehicles communicating false information should be enough to raise a few eyebrows.

Despite all these risks, security and privacy have not been ignored by NHTSA. "As a networked system, V2V/V2I are intended to employ a secure and reliable communications network, allow only certified devices to access that network, and have a trusted entity (the Security Certificate Management System) to issue, distribute, and, when necessary, revoke device certificates."[59] However, digital certificate systems by and of themselves can contain vulnerabilities. Although Security Certificate Management Systems are slightly different because they deal with certifying devices rather than a user's identity, both share common features such as the reliance on Certificate Authorities. Furthermore, "[d]igital certificates have become one of the latest targets, especially with enterprises relying

---

[57] *Id.*
[58] *Supra* note 1.
[59] *Supra* note 47.

on certificates more than ever to keep system connections secure."[60]

One vulnerability is caused by the Certificate Authority or the company managing the certificates. Poor management of these certificates is a "primary vulnerability."[61] "The problem is that Certificate Authorities "CAs" can be compromised, as exemplified by incidents at certificate authorities such as DigiNotar, Comodo and DigiCert."[62] Even worse, "if an attacker can usurp control of a certificate, forge a certificate or compromise a certificate, all the benefits offered are made moot."[63] Furthermore, "[t]here are hundreds of CAs issuing digital trust worldwide and the average organization has over 23,000 keys and certificates, according to Ponemon Institute research. When a major CA is breached or when a CA fraudulently issues unauthorized certificates for an organization, attackers can impersonate, surveil and monitor their organizational targets, as well as decrypt traffic and impersonate websites, code or administrators."[64] "If the certificate private key is compromised, the entire PKI environment is compromised."[65]

---

[60] Frank OhlHorst,, *The Hidden Threats of Security Certificates*, BASELINE MAG. (Dec. 4 2012), http://www.baselinemag.com/security/the-hidden-threats-of-security-certificates (last accessed March 6, 2018).
[61] *Id.*
[62] *Id.*
[63] *Id.*
[64] Warwick Ashford, *Security pros failing to address digital certificate risks, survey shows*, COMPUTER WEEKLY (Sep. 9, 2015), http://www.computerweekly.com/news/4500253143/Security-pros-failing-to-address-digital-certificate-risks-survey-shows.
[65] Gemalto, *Latest Breaches Expose PKI's Greatest Weakness – Encryption Keys*, (Sep. 22, 2011), http://www.sentinelcloud.com/About/NewsMedia/PKIs-Greatest-

NHTSA touts that its V2V security system complies with NIST standards. However, compliance does not equate to security. A primary example of this was the Target data breach and subsequent theft of consumer information. [66] Target at the time of the breach was compliant with Payment Card Information security standards, yet their security was compromised through the HVAC system. [67] Furthermore, the MITRE Corporation already identified 21 "high-level threats" to the V2V security system in its 2015 technical report to the Department of Transportation.[68]

In a study on Cooperative Adaptive Cruise Control ("CACC") vehicle streams, which employ V2V communication, researchers identified several forms of possible attacks with varying effects on the vehicles in the stream. The researchers pointed to the insider vulnerability which could "cause significant instability in the CACC

Weakness–Encryption-Keys/ (last accessed March 6, 2018).

[66] *See generally* John P. Mello Jr., *Target Breach Lesson: PCI Compliance Isn't Enough*, TECH NEWS WORLD (Mar. 18, 2014), available athttp://www.technewsworld.com/story/80160.html; Aviva Litan., *How PCI failed Target and U.S. Consumers*, GARTNER (Jan. 20, 2014), http://blogs.gartner.com/avivah-litan/2014/01/20/how-pci-failed-target-and-u-s-consumers/; Jaikumar Vijayan, *After Target, Neiman Marcus breaches, does PCI compliance mean anything?*, COMPUTER. WORLD (Jan. 24, 2014), http://www.computerworld.com/article/2486879/data-security/after-target--neiman-marcus-breaches--does-pci-compliance-mean-anything-.html.

[67] *Id.*

[68] MITRE Corporation, *Final Requirements Report*, Dept. of Transportation FHWA-JPO-15-235, ii (Sept. 11, 2015), https://www.regulations.gov/contentStreamer?documentId=NHTSA-2016-0126-0008&attachmentNumber=1&disposition=attachment&contentType=pdf.

vehicle stream."[69] Attacks discussed included "application layer, network layer, system level, and privacy leakage attacks."[70] The researchers explained "[a]ll these attacks can potentially impact the string stability of the system and compromise the safety and privacy of the passengers of the CACC vehicle stream. Such attacks can be launched either by an outsider or insider adversary."[71]

> "In the message falsification attack, the adversary starts listening to the wireless medium, and…manipulates the content…and rebroadcasts it… In the spoofing attack, the adversary impersonates another vehicle in the stream in order to inject fraudulent information into a specific vehicle….In a replay attack, the adversary receives and stores a beacon sent by a member of the stream and tries to replay it at a later point of time with malicious intent. The replayed beacon contains old information which can lead to hazardous effects…the adversary can attempt a Denial-of- Service…attack to overwhelm the communication capability of a vehicle or a group of vehicles, and make them unable to participate properly in a CACC vehicle stream. A known method…is by using a vehicular botnet. Radio jamming to deliberately disrupt communications over small or wide geographic areas…is another possible network layer DoS attack….Another type of attack is tampering with vehicle hardware or

---

[69] Mani Amoozadeh,et al., *Security Vulnerabilities of Connected Vehicles Streams and their Impact on Cooperative Driving*, 53 IEEE Communications Magazine 6 126, 126 (June 2015), http://ieeexplore.ieee.org/document/7120028/?reload=true.
[70] *Id.*
[71] *Id.* at 127.

software…done by a malicious insider in the manufacturing level or by an outsider in an unattended vehicle (for instance by replacing or altering certain vehicle sensors). Even if the communication channel is secure, and a state-of-the-art security architecture is deployed…if the on-board hardware/software are tampered with or faulty, then the input information to the system will not be accurate."[72]

The study goes on to note the privacy implications of eavesdropping on the vehicle's CACC stream. "CACC vehicles periodically broadcast beacons that contain[] various information such as the vehicle identity, current vehicle position, speed, acceleration, etc. The availability of this information can compromise…privacy."[73] Such information as position, speed, and acceleration data falls under required data in NHTSA's NPRM. The chart below is from the above study and provides a visual understanding of the types of attacks that may be exercised on a vehicle communication stream such as DSRC.

---

[72] *Id.* at 127-128.
[73] *Id.* at 128.

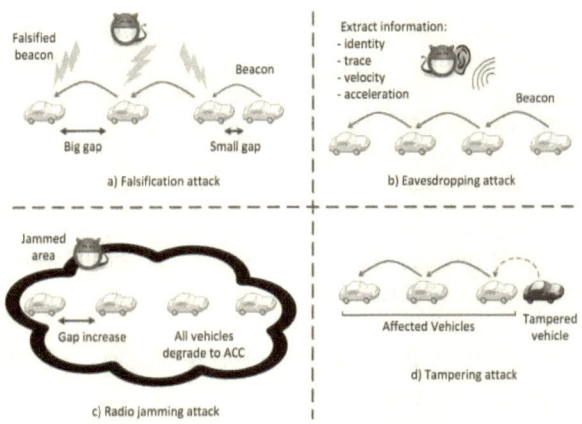

Fig. 2. Security attacks on a CACC vehicle stream.[74]

II.   VEHICLE TO VEHICLE COMMUNICATIONS INTER-AGENCY
       WORKING GROUP

"This is what happens when you put one of every kind of scientist in a room [with] a laser junky."[75] Intellectual Venture Labs, funded by Bill Gates, developed a solution to fight malaria that identified mosquitoes which were prone to carry the disease and remove their wings using a targeted laser. This technology would be applied in a square formation surrounding a village or home, effectively creating a protective net around communities.[76] As

---

[74] *Id.* at 132.

[75] Pablos Holman, *Top Hacker Shows Us How it's Done.* TEDXMIDWEST (Aug. 30 2012), https://www.youtube.com/watch?v=hqKafl7Amd8. *See also, Photonic Fence,* INTELLECTUAL VENTURES, http://www.intellectualventures.com/inventions-patents/our-inventions/photonic-fence/ (last visited Jan. 30 2017).

[76] *Photonic Fence, supra* note 75.

Intellectual Venture Labs notes on their website approximately 600,000 people die annually from malaria.[77]

The development and application of this laser-based technology was no small feat.[78] It was primarily successful due to the collaboration of scientists from many different fields. This notion of collaboration breeding innovation applies with equal force to the challenges and opportunities presented by connected cars.

A. Emerging Technologies and Interagency Working Groups

Some have already advocated for new authorities to "aid the safe deployment of new technologies,"[79] and inter-agency working groups have been utilized to address scenarios like those presented by connected cars. For example, one was formed to address differing aspects of drone policy, including the domestic use of unmanned aerial systems by federal law enforcement [80] and the prohibited use

---

[77] *Id.*

[78] Holman, *supra* note 75.

[79] Press Release, Rep. Dan Lipinski, D., Rep. Lipinski Reacts to DOT Autonomous Car Recommendations (Sep. 20, 2016) (https://lipinski.house.gov/press-releases/rep-lipinski-reacts-to-dot-autonomous-car-recommendations/). *See also* NHTSA, FEDERAL AUTOMATED VEHICLES POLICY, (Sep. 2016), https://www.transportation.gov/AV/federal-automated-vehicles-policy-september-2016.

[80] DEPT. OF JUST. POL'Y GUIDANCE, DOMESTIC USE OF UNMANNED AIRCRAFT SYSTEMS, https://www.justice.gov/file/441266/download.

> The Department's working group was led by the Office of Legal Policy and included the Department's Chief Privacy and Civil Liberties Officer and representatives of the Bureau of Alcohol, Tobacco, Firearms and Explosives, the Criminal Division, the

of drones during wildfires.[81]   Another was formed under the Department of Justice to study the department's own domestic use of drones.   Ultimately, the working groups resulted in policy guidance that set forth principles to protect privacy and civil rights stemming from the use of drones.[82]

Many other examples of successful working groups exist, with goals including the improvement of drone policy and Internet of Things technologies, of which connected cars are a part. The 2015 White House Presidential Memorandum on   Promoting   Economic   Competitiveness   While Safeguarding Privacy, Civil Rights, and Civil Liberties in Domestic Use of Unmanned Aircraft Systems was a result

---

Office of Community Oriented Policing, the Civil Rights Division, the Office of the Deputy Attorney General, the Drug Enforcement Administration, the Federal Bureau of Investigation, the National Security Division, the Executive Office for United States Attorneys, the Office of Justice Programs, the Office of Privacy and Civil Liberties, the United States Marshals Service, and the Office of the Chief Information Officer.
Id.

[81] The Editor, *Federal Agencies Working Together to Combat Unauthorized Drone Use During Wildfire Operations*, UAS VISION (June 14, 2016), http://www.uasvision.com/2016/06/14/federal-agencies-working-together-to-combat-unauthorized-drone-use-during-wildfire-operations/ (explaining "the National Wildfire Coordinating Group, an interagency body of senior fire officials from federal and state wildland fire management organizations, established improved drone incursion notification protocols for wildland firefighters.").
[82] *2015 White House Presidential Memorandum: Promoting Economic Competitiveness While Safeguarding Privacy, Civil Rights, and Civil Liberties in Domestic Use of Unmanned Aircraft Systems*, (Feb. 2015), https://www.whitehouse.gov/the-press-office/2015/02/15/presidential-memorandum-promoting-economic-competitiveness-while-safegua.

of federal interagency collaboration.[83] The Inter-Agency Working Group on Facilities and Infrastructure also formed a Task Force on Unmanned Systems which advised the group on policy and plans related to the use of "Autonomous Underwater Vehicles (AUV), Gliders, Unmanned Aircraft Systems (UAS), Unmanned Surface Vessels (USV) and Lagrangian Platforms."[84]

Another example is the Networking and Information Technology Research and Development Program which consists of several interagency working groups that address research in emerging areas such as the Internet of Things.[85] The Program includes more than a dozen working groups covering research in program areas including:

> "Big Data, Cyber Physical Systems, Cyber Security and Information Assurance, Human

---

[83] *Id. See also* Allyn K. Milojevich, *Proliferation of Unmanned Aerial Systems (Drones) and Policy Challenges on the Horizon: A Policy Memorandum to John P. Holdren*, 8 J. OF SCIENCE, POLICY, AND GOVERNANCE 1 (Feb. 2016) http://www.sciencepolicyjournal.org/uploads/5/4/3/4/5434385/milojevi ch_proliferationofdrones.pdf (proposing an interagency working group to develop a comprehensive framework for drone policy). *See also, Lisa Ellman, '05: Polivation Expert Leads at White House and in Drone Policy*, UNIVERSITY OF CHICAGO LAW SCHOOL (Apr. 5 2016), https://www.law.uchicago.edu/news/lisa-ellman-05-polivation-expert-leads-white-house-and-drone-policy (involvement in federal interagency working group on drone policy).

[84] *Interagency Working Group on Facilities and Infrastructure (IWG-FI)*, NAT'L OCEANOGRAPHIC PARTNERSHIP PROGRAM, http://www.nopp.org/about-nopp/committees/iwg-fi/ (last visited Jan. 7, 2017).

[85] Bruce, Correa & Subramanyam, *Internet of Things: Examining Opportunities and Challenges*, WHITE HOUSE BLOG (Aug. 30, 2016), https://www.whitehouse.gov/blog/2016/08/30/internet-things-examining-opportunities-and-challenges.

> Computer Interaction and Information Management, High Confidence Software and Systems, Health Information Technology Research and Development, High End Computing, Large Scale Networking, Joint Engineering Team, Middleware And Grid Interagency Coordination Team, Privacy Research & Development, Robotics and Intelligent Systems, Social Computing, Software Productivity, Sustainability, and Quality, Video and Image Analytics, Wireless Spectrum Research and Development."[86]

The National Institute of Standards and Technology also formed an Inter-Agency Working group to address the growth and expansion of the Internet of Things.[87]

When established, many working groups seek input and collaboration from a variety of sources, including other regulatory agencies. Not only have Inter-Agency Working Groups been formed to address these emerging technologies but the FCC has already collaborated with the Department of Transportation previously to address problems caused by emerging technologies. The Agencies previously collaborated on an issue caused by the increase in consumer cell phones and subsequent use of these devices on aircraft. The Agencies sought to continue the "safe and secure use of

---

[86] *NITRD Coordination Areas*, NETWORKING AND INFO. TECH. RESEARCH AND DEV. PROGRAM, https://www.nitrd.gov/nitrdgroups/index.php?title=Subcommittee_on_ Networking_and_Information_Technology_Research_and_Developme nt_(NITRD_Subcommittee) (last visited Jan. 7, 2017).

[87] *CPS Public Working Group*, NIST, https://pages.nist.gov/cpspwg/ (last visited January 7, 2017). *See also* Bruce, Correa & Subramanyam, supra note 85.

consumer communications technology onboard domestic commercial aircraft."[88]

Each working group is uniquely created and has a unique purpose; however, all successful collaborations share certain commonalities. Several characteristics in particular have been identified as indicia of future success.

These approaches included "defining outcomes, measuring performance, and ensuring accountability, establishing leadership approaches, [and] using resources such as funding, staff, and technology" in overcoming collaborative challenges.[89] One key aspect of "defining outcomes" is to "start a group" that includes "the most directly affected participants" and "gradually broaden th[is] group to include other[]" affected or interested parties. When it comes to connected vehicle technology the most directly affected federal agencies include NHTSA, the FCC, and the FTC.[90]

If applied to connected cars, a working group comprised of the key federal stakeholders – including, for example, the FTC, FCC, and NHTSA – could not only address the privacy and security implications of connected vehicle technology, but also resolve the ambiguity presented by overlapping regulatory jurisdictions.[91]

---

[88] FCC, *FCC Announces Agreement with the U.S. Department of Transportation Establishing a Framework for Coordination of Aviation Communications Safety and Security Issues*, (Jan. 29, 2016), https://apps.fcc.gov/edocs_public/attachmatch/DA-16-110A1_Rcd.pdf.

[89] Veal et al., *Practical Approaches for Implementing Successful Collaborative Groups*, THE PUBLIC MANAGER (Sept. 15, 2014), https://www.td.org/Publications/Magazines/The-Public-Manager/Archives/2014/Fall/Practical-Approaches-for-Implementing-Successful-Collaborative-Groups.

[90] The FTC, NHTSA, and the FCC are the most directly affected parties based upon their jurisdiction and regulatory missions.

[91] Turrecha, Pulliam & Bruno, *FTC Drives Autonomous Car Reg*

B. Joint Policymaking by the FTC, FCC, and NHTSA

President Obama once joked "[t]he Interior Department is in charge of salmon while they're in freshwater, but the Commerce Department handles them when they're in saltwater. I hear it gets even more complicated once they're smoked." [92] Joint rulemaking provides a solution to this issue of overlapping jurisdiction and involves varying techniques from "following model rules" to the use of "interlocking" and "parallel" rules" and the "adoption of another agency's rules as reference." [93] However, "the best example[s] of such an instrument is joint rulemaking, which typically involves two or more agencies agreeing to adopt a single regulatory preamble and text." [94]

> "Agencies appear to use joint rulemaking on an ad hoc basis to promote uniformity primarily where they perform closely related regulatory missions and where Congress has allocated each of them a role implementing one or a set of related statutes…in certain cases, the agencies jointly promulgating rules do not generally work

---

Toward Privacy and Security, LEXOLOGY (Nov. 23 2016), http://www.lexology.com/library/detail.aspx?g=f3686e39-1e13-42fd-9ff0-2afa2e5a119e ("The constant slew of innovations and advancements in smart cars has so far left regulators struggling to define new rules to govern this space. The overlapping jurisdictions of three different agencies - …NHTSA, the…FTC, and the…FCC) – with different priorities have only added to the complexity.").

[92] Freeman & Rossi, *Improving Interagency Coordination in Shared Regulatory Space*, 38 ADMIN. & REG. L. NEWS 11, 11 (2013).

[93] Freeman & Rossi, *Agency Coordination in Shared Regulatory Space*, 125 HARV. L. REV. 1131, 1165-66 (Mar. 2012).

[94] *Id.* at 1166-67.

on related issues, yet they share an interest in implementing one particular law."[95]

Such joint rulemaking efforts, although accounting for a minimal amount of total annual rules,[96] have been successful in the past [97] and address the current context most appropriately. The FTC, NHTSA, and the FCC "perform closely related regulatory missions,"[98] "Congress has allocated each of them a role implementing…related statutes"[99] and all "share an interest" in the implementation of connected vehicle technology. Furthermore, such joint policymaking efforts "tend to be more visible and legally enforceable then interagency agreements."[100] In an area where security and privacy are prevalent such visibility and enforceability is tantamount to the success of connected vehicle technology.

---

[95] *Id.* 1167-1168.

[96] *Id.* at 1167.

[97] *Id.* at 1169 (referring to joint EPA-NHTSA rule and Dodd-Frank Act joint rulemaking requirements).

[98] 47 U.S.C. § 151 (2017) ("for the purpose of promoting safety of life and property through the use of wire and radio communications."); 49 U.S.C. § 30101 (2013) ("to reduce traffic accidents and deaths and injuries resulting from traffic accidents."); 15 U.S.C § 45(a) (2012) ("Unfair methods of competition in or affecting commerce, and unfair or deceptive acts or practices in or affecting commerce, are hereby declared unlawful.").

[99] *E.g.*, Markey, *supra* note 48 (the FCC in implementing licensing and servicing rules for the 5.9ghz bandwidth). 49 U.S.C. § 30101 (2013) (NHTSA in implementing DSRC as "motor vehicle equipment" which utilizes this bandwidth to operate). 15 U.S.C § 45(a) (2012) (the FTC in preventing possible "unfair trade practices" using data created by this system.).

[100] Turrecha, Pulliam & Bruno, *supra* note 90, at 1166. *See also* Freeman & Rossi, *supra* note 91, at 12.

One of the great benefits of such joint policy making is the capability to "adopt[] another agency's rules as reference."[101] NHTSA has spent a respectable and considerable amount of time developing V2V and V2I communication systems. The benefit of joint rulemaking will allow adopting of NHTSA's current rules as a foundation from which to begin further collaboration. This will also help alleviate auto manufacturers concerns regarding delay of the technology as well as provide them additional time to prepare for the mandate. Examples of successful joint rulemaking efforts NHSTA has engaged in the past include a joint rule on greenhouse gas emissions formed in conjunction with the Environmental Protection Agency.[102]

NHTSA and the Environmental Protection Agency could have tried to issue compatible rules. However, going through the process of joint rulemaking "made the prospect of successful harmonization much more likely. According to a GAO report reviewing the process, the agencies worked much more closely together than ever before, sharing responsibility for the rule from preamble to conclusion."[103] Other regulations such as the Dodd-Frank Act go so far as to "require[] joint rulemaking in many provisions" due to the overlapping jurisdictional nature of financial regulation. These requirements serve to "minimize potentially inconsistent regulations" while "manag[ing] numerous overlaps" in the sector of financial regulation.[104]

Applied to connected cars, the different expertise of the NHTSA, FTC, and FCC would produce more well-

---

[101] Turrecha, Pulliam & Bruno, *supra* note 91.
[102] *Id.* at 1169.
[103] *Id.* at 1172-73.
[104] *Id.* at 1168.

rounded regulations. As Freeman and Rossi explain "[o]verlapping delegations are not always inefficient. They can create distinct advantages, including the potential to harness the expertise and competencies of specialized agencies."[105]

As to connected vehicle technology, such a benefit could be realized by allowing decision making to be led by the agency whose expertise and jurisdiction best fit the particular section of the rule in question. For example, decisions on the collection and use of data gathered would be led by the FTC. Decisions regarding the security of the overall communications system, the 5.9ghz bandwidth, would be led by the FCC. Decisions regarding the vehicle itself, such as malware spreading to other systems on the car, would be led by the NHTSA. Despite these possible specializations, all agencies would have the opportunity and discretion to collaborate and make decisions on the holistic framework to ensure its overall suitability to the solution.[106]

---

[105] Freeman & Rossi, *supra* note 92.

[106] An Inter-Agency Working Group would also mitigate the danger of so-called regulatory capture. Ralph Nader framed the issue in a different automobile context: "[w]hile GM's defective parts killed people when air bags failed to open, NHTSA failed when its investigations failed to open despite repeated warnings of deadly problems…Its passive approach to the companies it is supposed to regulate…fits the textbook definition of "regulatory capture"." Identification of regulatory capture can be complicated, often only identifiable by the public with the benefit of hindsight. However, the solution to prevent this risk from coming to fruition is the inter-agency working group model. Ralph Nader, *Safety in name only at NHTSA*, USA TODAY (Sep. 17, 2014), http://www.usatoday.com/story/opinion/2014/09/17/ralph-nader-safety-nhtsa-investigation-regulation-congress-gm-stalled-column/15801047/. "A report from the House Energy and Commerce committee…found that NHTSA's incompetence played a role in allowing the General Motors ignition switch crisis to go undetected for years, and says that

GAO reports on NHTSA also establish some concern as to their ability to regulate this area alone.[107]

C.   Why the FCC?

If the proposal for an inter-agency working group is to be followed, its composition is critical. The FCC has extensive experience working on cybersecurity and privacy issues.[108] DSRC uses the 5.9GHz bandwidth which "the FCC is responsible for the entirety of"[109] and "the FCC's

---

the agency continues to lag behind in its efforts to improve its performance." *See* STAFF REPORT ON THE GM IGNITION SWITCH RECALL: REVIEW OF NHTSA U.S. H.R. COMM. ON ENERGY AND COMMERCE, (Sep. 16, 2014), http://energycommerce.house.gov/sites/republicans.energycommerce.house.gov/files/Hearings/OI/20140915GMFootnotes/NHTSAreportfinal.pdf.

[107] The United States Government Accountability Office found that NHTSA did not have the critical knowledge and expertise in security or privacy that is needed to protect the auto industry from cyber threats. "NHTSA itself state[d] that it will not have a clear position on whether there is even a need for cybersecurity standards in vehicles until 2018." Furthermore, "[T]he culture of the car industry encourages bad behavior on privacy, lax cybersecurity, discourages auto manufacturers from publicizing and sharing information on potential vulnerabilities, and erects barriers to the ability of auto manufacturers to push out timely cybersecurity updates." Open Technology Institute & Public Knowledge, *Petition for Rulemaking and Request for Emergency Stay of Operation of Dedicated Short-Range Communications Service in the 5.850-5.9925 GHZ Band (5.9 GHZ Band)*, iv (June 28, 2016).

[108] Electronic Privacy Information Center, Comment Letter on Federal Motor Vehicle Safety Standards: Vehicle-to-Vehicle (V2V) Communications (Oct. 20, 2014), https://epic.org/apa/comments/EPIC-NHTSA-V2V-Comments.pdf.

[109] *Understanding the Difference Between NHTSA and the FCC's Definitions of DSRC*, PUBLIC KNOWLEDGE 2, https://www.publicknowledge.org/assets/uploads/documents/1Pager_-

service rules for the band serve as the backdrop against which NHTSA's DSRC standards are deployed. Th[ese] service rules govern basics of the safety services…as well as any noncommercial services deployed in the majority of the band."[110] In allocating the 5.850-5.925 GHz spectrum for DSRC devices, the FCC reserved the right to take "whatever action is necessary to implement the standards related to DSRC use."[111]

The FCC is also heavily focused on cybersecurity and has aggressively sought to protect the privacy[112] and security of consumers. In 2014, the FCC fined two telecommunications companies $10 million dollars for not protecting consumer's financial data.[113] At the time FCC

_NHTSA_vs_FCC_DSRC.pdf.

[110] *Id.*

[111] *In the Matter of Amendment of Parts 2 and 90 of the Commission's Rules to Allocate the 5.850-5.925 GHz Band to the Mobile Service for Dedicated Short Range Communications of Intelligent Transportation Services, Report and Order*, ET Docket No. 98-95, 14 FCC Rcd. 18221 (1999) (explaining "[w]e defer consideration of licensing and service rules and spectrum channelization plans to a later proceeding because standards addressing such matters are still under development by the Department of Transportation. Once such standards are developed, the Commission could take whatever action is necessary to implement the standards related to DSRC use.").

[112] *See* Nat'l Cable & Telecommunications Ass'n v. Fed. Commc'n Comm'n, 555 F.3d 996 (D.C. Cir. 2009) (upholding the Commission's order for consent opt-in scheme in response to rise in third party data brokers). Note that automakers utilizing connected vehicle or wireless technology already store data, sometimes in third party data centers. *Supra* note 32.

[113] Press Release, Federal Communications Commission, FCC Plans $10M Fine For Carriers That Breached Consumer Privacy (Oct. 24, 2014), available at http://www.fcc.gov/document/10m-fine-proposed-against-terracom-and-yourtel-privacy-breaches. *See also* Brian Fung, *With a $10 million fine, the FCC is leaping into data security for the first time*, THE WASHINGTON POST (Oct. 24, 2014),

official Travis Leblanc warned it wouldn't be the last data security action by the FCC; additional enforcement actions have supported this posture[114] Furthermore, at a time when the FCC is refreshing the record on sharing techniques in the 5.850-5.925 GHz band that would allow commercial applications to utilize the bandwidth alongside life and safety systems[115] deployment of such devices at this time would present unique challenges.

More importantly, the FCC has jurisdiction over "wire and radio," including the 5.9 GHz bandwidth.[116] The FCC has a "broad scope of authority"[117] and therefore should have a role in regulating DSRC to fulfill its statutory

---

https://www.washingtonpost.com/news/the-switch/wp/2014/10/24/with-a-10-million-fine-the-fcc-is-leaping-into-data-security-for-the-first-time.

[114] *Id. See also* Fed. Commc'n Comm'n, *AT&T to Pay $25 Million To Settle Consumer Privacy Investigation: FCC's Largest Data Security Enforcement Action*, FCC, (Apr. 8, 2015), https://apps.fcc.gov/edocs_public/attachmatch/DOC-332911A1.pdf.

[115] *The Commission Seeks to Update and Refresh the Record in the "Unlicensed National Information Infrastructure (U_NII) Devices in the 5 GHz Band" Proceeding*, ET Docket No. 13-49, Public Notice, 31 FCC Rcd. 6130 (2016).

[116] 47 U.S.C. § 151 (2017).

[117] FCC v. Midwest Video Corp., 440 US 689, 696 (1979) (citing FCC v. Pottsville Broadcasting Co., 309 US 134, 138 (1940)) ("Congress meant to confer broad authority on the Commission...so as to "maintain through appropriate administrative control, a grip on the dynamic aspects of radio transmission""). *See also* Cooperative Comm. Inc. v. AT&T Corp., 867 F.Supp. 1151, 1516 (D. Utah 1994) (finding that "in enacting the Communications Act, it is manifest that Congress intended to occupy the field of telecommunications, in order to make available to all people of the United States a rapid, efficient, reasonably-priced communications service, governed by one uniform regulatory scheme" and holding that state tort law claims were not barred due to savings clause in Communications Act).

mandate.[118] Additionally, the FCC has ancillary jurisdiction over the "regulated subject" in question, i.e., DSRC devices using the 5.9GHz bandwidth.

D. Why The FTC?

The Federal Trade Commission has extensive experience in data security, bringing over 60 enforcement actions since 2002.[119] 50 of these actions led to settlements.[120] Jessica Rich, the Director of the Bureau of Consumer Protection explains that "data security enforcement remains a critical FTC priority"[121] and, as such,

---

[118] American Broadcasting Co. v. F.C.C., 191 F.2d 492, 498 (D.C. Cir. 1951) (reasoning "[t]he purpose of Congress in establishing the Commission was to set up an expert agency capable of coping with the ever-changing and constantly-increasing problems of a booming industry" and upholding Commission's authority to regulate broadcast frequency allocation but reversing Commission's orders on other grounds). *See also Pottsville*, *supra* note 117 at 138 ("Underlying the whole law is recognition of the rapidly fluctuating factors characteristic of the evolution of broadcasting and of the corresponding requirement that the administrative process possess sufficient flexibility to adjust itself to these factors").

[119] David Gerber, *FTC: Bad Cybersecurity Is an Unfair Trade Practice*, OFFIT KURMAN (Sept. 12, 2016), http://www.offitkurman.com/ftc-bad-cybersecurity-is-an-unfair-trade-practice/. *See also* Cases and Proceedings Advanced Search: Consumer Protection Data Security from January 1, 2002 to December 31, 2017 (duplicating this search on the FTC website will return the aforementioned results.)

[120] Soyong Cho & Andrew L. Caplan, *Cybersecurity Lessons Learned From the FTC's Enforcement History*, K & L GATES 2 (Dec. 2014), http://m.klgates.com/files/Publication/eeb01ded-7e7e-4e1a-a055-b50d1b66387a/Presentation/PublicationAttachment/46b8860d-63fd-48af-aaf0-bbfd00f7a9ed/Cybersecurity_Alert_122214.pdf.

[121] *Id.*

many have viewed the FTC as the "primary federal data security regulator."[122]

Another emerging technology that shows the potential benefits of the FTC's role on the proposed inter-agency working group is the Internet of Things. The FTC deals extensively with the Internet of Things which connects our world more every day. This year the largest distributed denial of service attack in history occurred with the aid of the Internet of Things. These devices provided for the formation of a botnet which sent approximately 665 Gb worth of packets each second towards the servers that ran the website Krebs on Security.[123] This is the equivalent of a hard drive on a modern laptop being completely filled with data every second. Another famous attack utilizing the botnet nicknamed Mirai took advantage of Internet of Things

---

[122] Ryan T. Bergsieker, Richard H. Cunningham & and Lindsey Young, *The Federal Trade Commission's Enforcement of Data Security Standards*, 44 THE COLO. LAW 39, 39 (2015). Furthermore, "FTC attention has regularly focused on data encryption. In more than half of cases requiring data or security programs, the FTC addressed the defendant's encryption protocols." Such experience would be useful in reviewing encryption methodologies used in Connected Vehicle Technology. The FTC's experience with connected technologies also speaks volumes about the possible benefit of their participation in rulemaking. *See* Patricia Bailin, *Study: What FTC Enforcement Actions Teach Us About the Features of Reasonable Privacy and Data Security Practices*, THE PRIVACY ADVISOR (Sept. 19, 2014), https://iapp.org/news/a/study-what-ftc-enforcement-actions-teach-us-about-the-features-of-reasonable-privacy-and-data-security-practices/.
[123] Brian Krebs, *KrebsOnSecurity Hit With Record DDoS*, KREBSONSECURITY (Sept. 21 2016), https://krebsonsecurity.com/2016/09/krebsonsecurity-hit-with-record-ddos/. *See also* Eduard Kovacs, *Brian Krebs' Blog Hit by 665 Gbps DDoS Attack*, SECURITY WEEK (Sept. 21, 2016), http://www.securityweek.com/brian-krebs-blog-hit-665-gbps-ddos-attack.

devices such as CCTV's and digital video recorders to flood and interrupt services provided by the domain name service provider Dyn.[124] As a result, many highly trafficked websites including Twitter and Spotify were unable to stay up and running.[125]

> "The FTC hasn't been silent on Internet of Things security. In a speech at the Consumer Electronics Show (CES) in 2015, Ramirez called on companies making IoT products to limit the data they collect and destroy it when it is no longer needed. Companies exploring the Internet of Things market should appoint a security lead to manage privacy and security issues during product development. And IoT product companies should clearly explain to consumers when their data is being sold to marketing firms or used in ways they may not expect, Ramirez recommended.... The FTC under Ramirez has been among the most aggressive federal agencies in addressing the security and privacy challenges of the IoT. In addition to sponsoring conferences to discuss the impact of connected devices, the agency has put its foot forward to enforce laws about the collection and sharing of geolocation information. It has also issued fines to companies

---

[124] Paul, *Lawmakers to FTC: Do Something about Internet of Things Security*, SECURITY LEDGER (Nov. 8, 2016), https://securityledger.com/2016/11/lawmakers-to-ftc-do-something-about-internet-of-things-security/. *See also* Letter from Frank Pallone Jr., Member, Comm. on Energy and Commerce, Jan Schakowsky, Member, Subcomm. on Commerce, Mfg., and Trade, to Edith Ramirez, Chairwoman, Fed. Trade Comm'n (Nov. 3, 2016).
[125] *Id.*

that fail to properly secure their technology, resulting in harm to consumers."[126]

The FTC even sponsored a 25,000 prize competition aimed at developing "a tool that can be used against security vulnerabilities in Internet of Things systems."[127] "At its Internet of Things workshop in November 2013, the Commission specifically examined privacy and security issues relating to the different technologies involved with connected cars, including Event Data Recorders ("EDRs") and other vehicle telematics."[128] Based on this 2013

---

[126] *Id.*

[127] Fed. Trade Comm'n, *FTC Announces Internet of Things Challenge to Combat Sec. Vulnerabilities in Home Devices*, FTC (Jan. 4, 2017), https://www.ftc.gov/news-events/press-releases/2017/01/ftc-announces-internet-things-challenge-combat-security. *See also* Patrick Thibodeau, *FTC sets $25,000 prize for automatic IoT patching*, COMPUTER WORLD (Jan. 4, 2017), http://www.computerworld.com/article/3154348/security/ftc-sets-25-000-prize-for-automatic-iot-patching.html.

[128] Fed. Trade Comm'n, Comment Letter In the Matter of Advanced Notice of Proposed Rulemaking Regarding Federal Motor Vehicle Safety Standards: Vehicle-to-Vehicle Communications (Oct. 20, 2014), https://www.ftc.gov/system/files/documents/advocacy_documents/federal-trade-commission-comment-national-highway-traffic-safety-administration-regarding-nhtsa/141020nhtsa-2014-0022.pdf.

> [P]articipants described three general types of potential privacy and security risks arising from this connectivity. First, participants expressed concern about the ability of connected car technology to track consumers' precise geolocation over time . Such information may divulge personal details about an individual. Did Consumer A visit an AIDS clinic last Tuesday? What place of worship does he attend?...Second, FTC workshop participants expressed a concern that information about driving habits could be used to price insurance premiums or

Workshop[129] the FTC released a staff report "summari[zing] the workshop and provid[ing] staff[] recommendations in this area."[130] One recommendation is to incorporate security by design at the beginning of the product life cycle. The Commission recommends a few steps to achieve this including utilizing privacy and risk assessments, minimizing collection of data, and testing security measures before launch of the IoT product. The Commission also recommends training of employees in security, hiring of outside companies that have the capability to maintain "reasonable security," use of the defense in depth approach to protect identified risks, use of access control mechanisms to prevent unauthorized access, and finally monitoring of the product through its life cycle including the patching of vulnerabilities.[131]

The FTC has already contributed valuable input to NHTSA's ANPRM, including: "three primary concerns relating to V2V communications...The ability of connected car technology to track consumers' precise geolocation over

---

set prices for other auto-related products....A third concern relates to the security of connected cars. At the Commission's Internet of Things workshop, one participant discussed his successful efforts to remotely access a car's internal computer network; he reported that he was able to control the vehicle's brakes and other critical functionality by hacking into the telematics unit.
Id.

---

[129] FTC, THE INTERNET OF THINGS: PRIVACY & SECURITY IN A CONNECTED WORLD, (2015), https://www.ftc.gov/system/files/documents/reports/federal-trade-commission-staff-report-november-2013-workshop-entitled-internet-things-privacy/150127iotrpt.pdf.
[130] *Id.* at i.
[131] *Id.* at iii.

time; Information about driving habits used to price insurance premiums or set prices...and [t]he security of connected cars, including the ability for third-parties to remotely access a car's internal computer network."[132]

III.   JURISDICTIONAL ANALYSIS

   A. Radio is the FCC's Jurisdiction

      1. Purpose of The FCC

The FCC was created "[f]or the purpose of regulating interstate and foreign commerce in communication by wire and radio...for the purpose of promoting safety of life and property through the use of wire and radio communications, and for the purpose of securing a more effective execution of this policy by centralizing authority...granted by law to several agencies and by granting additional authority with

---

[132] Kelley Drye & Warren LLP, *FTC supports NHTSA's approach to privacy in V2V rulemaking*, LEXOLOGY (Oct. 27, 2014), http://www.lexology.com/library/detail.aspx?g=ac560f3f-f245-4d9f-a18d-729b3c090b48. The FTC has since acknowledged that NHTSA appropriately addressed these concerns in their current NPRM. *Id.*

> The FTC also noted that...NHTSA designed the proposed V2V system to limit the data collected and stored to that which serves the intended safety purposes, and to ensure that the collected data cannot be used to identify a particular individual or vehicle. Lastly, with respect to the security of the collected data, the FTC supports the NHTSA's decision to help mitigate the potential for unauthorized access to data by keeping the V2V device separate from other onboard computers.
> *Id.*

respect to interstate and foreign commerce in wire and radio communication."[133] The D.C. Circuit Court in *American Broadcasting* explained the reasoning for Congress in creating the FCC was to establish an agency to be able to adapt to the "ever-changing and constantly-increasing problems of a booming industry."[134]

In *American Broadcasting*, the Court was faced with a dispute regarding broadcast frequency allocation. The case dealt with special service authorizations which allowed the FCC to grant a temporary license to broadcasters to transmit on a different frequency then the one they had been licensed to use.[135] The Court found no reason to hold that these licenses were outside the FCC's authority.[136] Instead, the Court wrote that Section 303(r) of the Communications Act of 1934 "contemplates that the Commission will take the lead in exploring the possibilities of radio, and we think unlikely that Congress had in mind a particular method to this end."[137] These "possibilities of radio" are constantly being explored and protected by the FCC.

Several offices within the FCC work to fulfill the FCC's purpose in regards to radio. Specifically, the Wireless Telecommunications Bureau "develops and executes policies and procedures for fast, fair licensing of all wireless services...amateur radio to mobile broadband services."[138]

---

[133] 47 U.S.C. § 151.

[134] *American Broadcasting Co.*, *supra* note 118 (reasoning "[t]he purpose of Congress in establishing the Commission was to set up an expert agency capable of coping with the ever-changing and constantly-increasing problems of a booming industry").

[135] *Id.*

[136] *Id.*

[137] *Id.*

[138] *Wireless Telecommunications,* FCC, https://www.fcc.gov/wireless-telecommunications.

The Office of Engineering and Technology "maintains the U.S. Table of Frequency Allocations, manages the Experimental Licensing and Equipment Authorization programs, regulates the operation of unlicensed devices, and conducts engineering and technical studies."[139]

2. Scope of Authority

The Communications Act of 1934 "expresse[d] a desire on the part of Congress to maintain ... a grip on the dynamic aspects of radio transmission. Underlying the whole law is recognition of the rapidly fluctuating factors characteristic of the evolution of broadcasting ... and of the corresponding requirement that the administrative process possess sufficient flexibility to adjust itself to these factors."[140] "[I]t is clear that Congress meant to confer "broad authority" on the Commission...so as "to maintain, through appropriate administrative control, a grip on the dynamic aspects of radio transmission."[141]

United States Telecom Ass'n v. Fed Commc'n Comm'n dealt with the scope of the FCC's statutory

---

[139] *Engineering & Technology*, FCC, https://www.fcc.gov/engineering-%26-technology. In 2003 in an effort to protect the safety of the American public the FCC "adopted a Report and Order establishing licensing and service rules for the Dedicated Short Range Communications Service in the...5.9 GHz band". The FCC also licenses the DSRC road units which allow vehicle to infrastructure communication. *See Dedicated Short Range Communications (DSRC) Service*, FCC, (last visited Mar. 12, 2007), http://wireless.fcc.gov/services/index.htm?job=service_home&id=dedicated_src.
[140] *FCC v. Pottsville,* 309 U.S. 134, 138 (1940).
[141] *FCC v. Midwest Video Corp.*, 440 US 689, 696 (1979) (explaining the broad scope of authority intended by Congress when creating the FCC in 1934).

authority. In *US Telecom*, the issue presented to the D.C. District Court was whether "broadband internet access service c[ould] be considered a telecommunications service" and therefore under the FCC's jurisdiction specifically in regard to its 2015 Open Internet Order.[142] Telecom argued that the FCC's 2015 Open Internet Order went "beyond the scope of whatever ambiguity [the statute] contains."[143] The Court reasoned "that the proper classification of broadband turns "on the factual particulars of how Internet technology works and how it is provided, questions *Chevron* leaves to the Commission to resolve in the first instance."[144]

DSRC technology falls under Title II regulation by the FCC. Under the Telecommunications Act of 1996,[145] a telecommunications service as opposed to an information service falls under more restrictive Title II regulation. A telecommunications service is defined as "the offering of telecommunications for a fee directly to the public, or to such classes of users as to be effectively available directly to the public, regardless of the facilities used."[146] An information service is defined as "the offering of a capability for generating, acquiring, storing, transforming, processing, retrieving, utilizing, or making available information via telecommunications."[147] Although one might reason that DSRC would be classified as an information service, since there is no fee for DSRC besides that which is added to the

---

[142] *United States Telecom Ass'n v. Fed. Commc'n Comm'n*, 825 F.3d 674, 730 (D.C. Cir. 2016) (upholding broadband internet access as a telecommunications service under FCC regulatory authority).
[143] *Id* at 702.
[144] *Id* at 701.
[145] Telecommunications Act of 1996, Pub. LA. No. 104-104, 110 Stat. 56 (1996).
[146] 47 U.S.C. §153(53).
[147] 47 U.S.C. §153(24).

cost of the car, there is a third category which was created by Congress. This category is called the telecommunications management exception, which "exempts from information service treatment—and thus treats as a telecommunications service — "any use [of an information service] for the management, control, or operation of a telecommunications system or the management of a telecommunications service."[148] Since DSRC would be utilized "for the management, control, or operation of a telecommunications system"[149] known as V2V communication DSRC falls under this exception and is thus subject to more restrictive common carrier regulation as a telecommunications service. This is important because it allows the FCC to exercise more authority in regulating DSRC.

Likewise, in *US Telecom*, the finding that broadband internet access was a telecommunications service subjected it to more restrictive common carrier regulation.[150] The Court majority upheld the agency's interpretation of broadband internet access services as a form of telecommunications service.[151]

Jurisdiction over wire and radio is expressly granted in the FCC's founding statute.[152] Unlike broadband internet access, regulating DSRC devices does not involve the reclassification of DSRC as radio. Even if it were to involve such reclassification, DSRC devices, like broadband internet access, provide "data to and from … endpoints."[153] Regardless, DSRC devices utilize the 5.9 GHz radio bandwidth which "the FCC is responsible for the entirety

---

[148] *United States Telecom Ass'n,* 825 F.3d at 691.

[149] *Id.*

[150] *Id* at 739.

[151] *Id* at 700.

[152] 47 U.S.C. § 151.

[153] *United States Telecom Ass'n, supra* note 142, at 696.

of"[154] and the rules for this band are the foundation "against which NHTSA's DSRC standards are deployed."[155] The FCC is obligated by its statutorily mandated responsibilities to "allocate the spectrum in a manner that promotes the "safety of life and property."[156] Furthermore, "under *City of Arlington*, the agency is entitled to deference even in matters concerning the scope of its own authority."[157]

> 3. In the Alternative, FCC has Ancillary Jurisdiction Over DSRC Technology

"The Commission recognized that it may exercise ancillary jurisdiction … when two conditions are satisfied: (1) the Commission's general jurisdictional grant under Title I covers the regulated subject and (2) the regulations are reasonably ancillary to the Commission's effective performance of its statutorily mandated responsibilities."[158] The FCC's "general jurisdiction grant" under Title I covers "wire and radio."[159] Therefore, the FCC's "general jurisdiction grant" covers "the regulated subject" or DSRC devices. The FCC was commissioned "for the purpose of promoting safety of life and property through the use of wire

---

[154] Public Knowledge, *supra* note 109, at 2.
[155] *Id.*
[156] Nat'l Assoc of Broadcasters v. FCC, 740 F.2d 1190, 1213 (D.C. Cir. 1984) (upholding Commission's decision to deregulate DBS systems).
[157] Christopher Wright, *The Scope of the FCC's Ancillary Jurisdiction After the D.C. Circuit Court's Net Neutrality Decisions*, 67 F. Comm's. L. J. 20, 34 (2015).
[158] American Library Assoc. v. FCC, 406 F. 3d 689, 691- 692 (D.C. Cir. 2005). Cited solely for purposes of laying out ancillary jurisdiction analysis. Case actually holds that the FCC exceeded their statutory authority regarding broadcast flag technology.
[159] 47 U.S.C. § 151.

and radio communications."[160] Thus, regulating DSRC devices are within the FCC's "statutorily mandated responsibility."

An opposing argument might point to the leading case *Comcast* where the Court found the FCC did not have ancillary jurisdiction.[161] However, that case was centered around the regulation of network management practices.[162] The Comcast Court explains "Courts have come to call the Commission's section 4(i) power its "ancillary" authority."[163] Section 4(i) provides that the Commission is authorized to "perform any and all acts, make such rules and regulations, and issue such orders, not inconsistent with this chapter, as may be necessary in the execution of its functions."[164] The *Comcast* Court notes that rejection of ancillary authority in all "three [leading Supreme Court] cases dealt with Commission jurisdiction over early cable systems at a time when the Communications Act gave the Commission no express authority to regulate such systems." [165] Contrary to these cases, Congress gave express authority over radio to the FCC.[166]

---

[160] *Id.*

[161] *Compare* Comcast Corp v. F.C.C., 600 F.3d 642, 644 (D.C. Cir. 2010) *with*, 47 U.S.C. § 151 (distinguishing from present issue where authority is explicitly provided for by Congress).

[162] *Comcast Corp.*, 600 F.3d at 644.

[163] *Id* at 646.

[164] 47 U.S.C. § 154(i).

[165] *Comcast* at 646; citing United States v. Southwestern Cable Co., 392 U.S. 157, 88 S.Ct. 1994, 20 L.Ed.2d 1001 (1968), United States v. Midwest Video Corp., 406 U.S. 649, 92 S.Ct. 1860, 32 L.Ed.2d 390 (1972) (Midwest Video I), and FCC v. Midwest Video Corp., 440 U.S. 689, 99 S.Ct. 1435, 59 L.Ed.2d 692 (1979) (Midwest Video II).

[166] 47 U.S.C. § 151.

4. The FCC's Interpretation of its Statutory Authority is Entitled to Chevron Deference

Chevron provides a two-step analysis for assessing whether an agency is afforded deference as to statutory interpretation. "First...is the question whether Congress has directly spoken to the precise question at issue. If the intent of Congress is clear, that is the end of the matter...[I]f the statute is silent or ambiguous with respect to the specific issue, the question for the court is whether the agency's answer is based on a permissible construction of the statute."[167]

Congress expressly provided that the FCC have jurisdiction over radio in the Communications Act of 1934. Assuming arguendo that such an intent is ambiguous as to DSRC, the FCC already regulates the bandwidth. Therefore, whether such an interpretation of its statutory authority is permissible has already been decided by previous regulation. As to the regulation of radio including Dedicated Short Range Communications the FCC is entitled to *Chevron* deference. Furthermore, "[u]nder *Chevron*...the FCC is entitled to substantial deference in its interpretation of the Communications Act, [and]...under *City of Arlington*, the agency is entitled to deference even in matters concerning the scope of its authority."[168]

---

[167] Chevron v. Natural Resources Defense Council, 467 U.S. 837, 842-43 (1984) (providing *Chevron* deference analysis).

[168] Wright, *supra* note 157, at 34. *See also* City of Arlington Tex, v. F.C.C., 133 S. Ct. 1863, 1866 (2013) ("We consider whether an agency's interpretation of a statutory ambiguity that concerns the scope of its regulatory authority (that is, its jurisdiction) is entitled to deference under Chevron. . .").

B. *FTC Jurisdiction in Support of Privacy of Individuals*

The Federal Trade Commission's authority over data security arises from "Section 5(a) of the Federal Trade Commission Act."[169] The Act prohibits "unfair or deceptive acts or practices in or affecting commerce."[170] This authority was affirmed in *Fed. Trade Comm'n v. Wyndham Worldwide Corp.*[171] The FTC alleged that Wyndham, a hospitality company, stored credit card information in unencrypted text, permitted use of simple passwords, and did not use firewalls

---

"It suffices to decide this case that the preconditions to deference under Chevron are satisfied because Congress has unambiguously vested the FCC with general authority to administer the Communications Act through rulemaking and adjudication, and the agency interpretation at issue was promulgated in the exercise of that authority. . . . Where Congress has established a clear line, the agency cannot go beyond it; and where Congress has established an ambiguous line, the agency can go no further than the ambiguity will fairly allow. But in rigorously applying the latter rule, a court need not pause to puzzle over whether the interpretive question presented is "jurisdictional." If "the agency's answer is based on a permissible construction of the statute," that is the end of the matter."
Id. at 1872.

[169] 15 U.S.C § 45(a) (2012).
[170] *Id.*
[171] Skelton Crystal, *FTC Data Security Enforcement: Analyzing the Past, Present, and Future*, COMPETITION J. 302, 303 (Spring 2016), http://www.kelleydrye.com/publications/articles/2079/_res/id=Files/index=0/Competition%20Journal%20Article%20by%20Crystal%20Skelton.pdf (citing Fed. Trade Comm'n v. Wyndham Worldwide Corp., 799 F.3d 236, 240 (3d Cir. 2015)).

to segregate its corporate and hotel property management networks from the internet contrary to the company's stated policy.[172] The Court held that the "company's alleged failure to maintain reasonable and appropriate data security…could constitute an unfair method of competition in commerce."[173]

"The FTC is the most active government enforcer with respect to business compliance with data security obligations."[174] Companies, such as auto manufacturers for example, "that accept consumers' personal data without reasonable and appropriate data security procedures to protect the data are considered by the Federal Trade Commission…to be engaging in unfair, and potentially deceptive, trade practices, in violation of 15 U.S.C. §§ 45(a) and (n) ("Section 45")."[175] Furthermore, if third party vendors do not use reasonable security measures the FTC may find the contracting company liable for the vendor's own lack of security measures [176] "In several cases, the FTC has alleged that the defendant was responsible for the security deficiencies of its third-party clients or end-users of its products or services."[177] An example of such third-party vendors in the context of the connected vehicle technology mandate would include the certificate authorities on which the system depends. The data created by connected vehicle technology in general could eventually be subject to the same standards as other personal consumer data. The FTC's collaborative input and expertise is likely to ensure that auto

---

[172] Fed. Trade Comm'n v. Wyndham Worldwide Corp., 799 F.3d 236, 241 (3d Cir. 2015).

[173] *Id.* at 236.

[174] *Skelton, supra* note 171, at 303.

[175] Gerber, *supra* note 119.

[176] Cho & Caplan, *supra* note 120.

[177] *Id.*

manufacturers have a clear yet affective standard to which they can adhere.

It is important to note that while the FTC has enforcement authority for unfair and deceptive trade practices their rulemaking authority is more limited. The FTC's rulemaking authority extends to the "use [of] trade regulation rules to remedy unfair or deceptive practices that occur on an industry-wide basis."[178] "Under Section 18 of the FTC Act, 15 U.S.C. Sec. 57a, the Commission is authorized to prescribe "rules which define with specificity acts or practices which are unfair or deceptive.""" [179] However, "before commencing a rulemaking proceeding the Commission must have reason to believe that the practices to be addressed by the rulemaking are "prevalent"."[180] In order to engage in rulemaking related to the V2V mandate the FTC would have to do so by specifying unfair or deceptive acts and practices related to DSRC. Furthermore, such rulemaking would have to address unfair or deceptive practices which are prevalent. However, throughout V2V rulemaking the FTC's comments have proven helpful and continued collaboration through an Inter-Agency Working Group is likely to yield similar results despite the FTC's admittedly limited authority regarding V2V rulemaking. With regard to enforcement for deceptive acts and practices involving data security the FTC's enforcement authority is well established.

---

[178] FTC, *A Brief Overview of the Federal Trade Commission's Investigative and Law Enforcement Authority* FCC (July 2008), https://www.ftc.gov/about-ftc/what-we-do/enforcement-authority.
[179] *Id.*
[180] *Id.* (citing 15 U.S.C. § 57a(b)(3)).

1. Deceptive Practices

"Early FTC data security cases relied almost exclusively on allegations of deceptive trade practices based on security practices inconsistent with representations companies made in their privacy policies or elsewhere."[181] Generally, "[t]he FTC will consider an act or practice to be deceptive "if there is a representation, omission, or practice that is likely to mislead the consumer acting reasonably in the circumstances, to the consumer's detriment."[182] "In the data security context, the FTC generally finds an act deceptive if an entity makes materially misleading statements...or deceptive omissions of material facts concerning its security measures and how it would handle, protect, or otherwise treat personal information that is inconsistent with the entity's actions."[183]

The amount of the FTC's consent decrees regarding misrepresentation and the misleading of consumers about the security or quality of their products speaks further to their competence and experience in data security.[184] As

---

[181] *FTC Data Security Standards and Enforcement*, Practical Law Intellectual Property & Technology, Resource ID 8-617-7036.
[182] Jennifer Woods, *Federal Trade Commission's Privacy and Data Security Enforcement Under Section 5*, https://www.americanbar.org/groups/young_lawyers/publications/the_1 01_201_practice_series/federal_trade_commissions_privacy.html.
[183] *Id. See also* 15 U.S.C. § 45(a) (2012); letter from Chairman Miller III, *FTC Policy Statement on Deception*, 1-2 (Oct. 14, 1984), https://www.ftc.gov/system/files/documents/public_statements/410531/ 831014deceptionstmt.pdf.
[184] In the Matter of ASUSTeK Computer, Inc., No. 142 3156, 2016 WL 807981, 37-44 (F.T.C. Feb. 22, 2016) (providing 4 counts for misrepresentations); In the Matter of Oracle Corp., No. 132 3115, 2016 WL 1360808, 3 (F.T.C. Mar 28, 2016) (explaining "Oracle represented, directly or indirectly, expressly or by implication, that by updating Java

aforementioned the Markey report discovered the majority of auto manufacturers offered technology features that gathered and sent data to a data center, sometimes run by a third party and explained further that "[c]ustomers [we]re often not explicitly made aware of data collection."[185] Such an omission in the context of connected vehicle technology could be considered deceptive practices in or affecting commerce. Although the FTC does not typically bring enforcement actions in the transportation sector[186] a review of *DOT Litigation News* reveals that NHTSA has not brought any enforcement actions in regards to data security practices by automakers.[187] The FTC may also pursue data security cases as unfair practices.

SE, Java users would ensure that Java SE on their computers had the latest security improvements. Oracle failed to disclose…in numerous instances, updating Java SE would not delete or replace all older iterations of Java SE…and as a result, a consumer's computer could still have iterations of Java SE installed that are vulnerable to security risks. This fact would be material to consumers' decision whether to take further action after "updating" Java SE to protect their computers."); In the Matter of Microsoft Corp., 134 F.T.C. 709, 2002 WL 34463137, 715 (F.T.C. Dec. 20, 2002) ("Passport did collect personally identifiable information other than that described in its privacy policy….the representation set forth in paragraph 15 was false or misleading.")

[185] *Supra* note 35.

[186] *FTC Data Security*, *supra* note 181.

[187] Office of General Counsel, *DOT Litigation News*, Department of Transportation https://www.transportation.gov/administrations/office-general-counsel/litigation-news, (last updated May, 6 2016) (reviewing March 2010 to March 2016).

2. Unfair Practices

The FTC has jurisdiction over "unfair...acts or practices in or affecting commerce."[188] "[T]he following three factors govern[] unfairness determinations: (1) whether the practice,... offends public policy...whether, in other words, it is within at least the penumbra of some common-law, statutory or other established concept of unfairness; (2) whether it is immoral, unethical, oppressive, or unscrupulous; [and] (3) whether it causes substantial injury to consumers (or competitors or other businessmen)." As noted by the Court in *Wyndham* "the Supreme Court implicitly approved these factors...acknowledging their applicability to contexts other than cigarette advertising and labeling."[189] "The Court also held that, under the policy statement, the FTC could deem a practice unfair based on the third prong—substantial consumer injury—without finding that at least one of the other two prongs was also satisfied."[190]

As to substantial injury to the consumer "[T}he FTC will deem an act or practice to be "unfair" if it (1) causes or is likely to cause substantial consumer injury (2) which is not reasonably avoidable by consumers themselves and (3) not outweighed by countervailing benefits to consumers and password maintenance to data collection and storage practices."[191] "The FTC's evaluation for an unfairness claim

---

[188] 15 U.S.C. §45(a)(1) (2012).

[189] *FTC v. Wyndham, supra* note 172, at 240.

[190] *Id.* at 243 ("§ 45(n) requires substantial injury that is not reasonably avoidable by consumers and that is not outweighed by the benefits to consumers or competition. It also acknowledges the potential significance of public policy and does not expressly require that an unfair practice be immoral, unethical, unscrupulous, or oppressive.")

[191] *Id.*

will generally focus on whether the practices at issue were "reasonable" under the circumstances and in light of industry standards, the cost and ease of having various security controls in place, and the known vulnerabilities of not having such controls."[192]

When considering data created by connected vehicle technology consumers have little control over how that data is used. Consumer injury resulting from the theft or manipulation of connected vehicle data would be "likely to cause substantial consumer injury", could not be "reasonably avoided by consumers themselves", and considering the availability of software to manage access to data such limited costs cannot "outweigh the countervailing benefits" to such consumers. As Senator Markey noted, "[c]ustomers [we]re often not explicitly made aware of data collection and, when they [we]re, they often cannot opt out without disabling valuable features, such as navigation."[193] Data on vehicle location and travel patterns could cause substantial consumer injury whether this data is used for more direct criminal purposes such as stalking, the targeting of homes for purposes of burglary,[194] or simply resale on the dark web to be used in identity theft.[195]

---

[192] *Id.*

[193] Markey, *supra* note 35.

[194] Beyoud, *supra* note 44.

[195] *See generally* Vindu Goel & Nicole Perlroth, *Hacked Yahoo Data Is for Sale on Dark Web*, N.Y. TIMES, Dec. 15, 2016, https://www.nytimes.com/2016/12/15/technology/hacked-yahoo-data-for-sale-dark-web.html?_r=0; James Connington, *How to check if your financial data is for sale on the dark web*, TELEGRAPH, Feb. 19, 2016, http://www.telegraph.co.uk/money/consumer-affairs/how-to-check-if-your-financial-data-is-for-sale-on-the-dark-web/; Arjun Kharpal, *Hackers are selling your data on the dark web...for only $1*, CNBC, Sept. 23, 2015, http://www.cnbc.com/2015/09/23/hackers-are-selling-your-data-on-the-dark-web-for-1.html.

The value of connected car data alone is valued around "$1.5 trillion by the year 2030 and it might even become a key focus area for the automotive industry."[196] This will draw attention from adversaries and lead to eventual breaches and subsequent theft of the data. As the mantra goes "it's not if, but when."[197] Therefore, it is paramount that auto companies are assured that their technologies including those mandated by NHTSA meet the data security standards provided not only by NHTSA but also those of the FTC. Consumers will not be the only ones who reap the benefits of a V2V Communications Inter-Agency Working Group.

IV.   CONCLUSION

The Supreme Court in *FCC v. Fox Television* held that "agency action is not subject to a heightened or more searching standard of review simply because it represents a change in administrative policy…[and] not every agency action representing a change in policy need be justified by reasons more substantial than those required to adopt a policy in the first instance."[198] Thus, if the FCC grants the

---

[196] Tim Clark, *Fasten Your Seat Belt, Connected Car Data Worth $1.5 Trillion*, FORBES, Sept. 7 2016, http://www.forbes.com/sites/sap/2016/09/07/fasten-your-seat-belt-connected-car-data-worth-1-5-trillion/#226876455a2b.

[197] *See generally*, BAE Systems, CyberSecurity Breaches: It's not if, but when, available at*https://www.baesystems.com/en/cybersecurity/cyber-security-breaches-its-not-if-but-when*

[198] F.C.C. v. Fox Television Stations, Inc., 556 U.S. 502, 513 (2009) (explaining that "our opinion in *State Farm* neither held nor implied that every agency action representing a policy change must be justified by reasons more substantial than those required to adopt a policy in the first instance. That case, which involved the rescission of a prior

petition for Emergency Stay and undertakes Rulemaking, their decision to act requires only the same reasons that would be necessary to "adopt a policy" of regulating radio "in the first instance."[199] Applying the same reasoning the FTC could also argue for jurisdiction over V2V and other autonomous technologies. As the District Court of New Jersey noted in *F.T.C. v. Wyndham Worldwide Corp.*, "even accepting that the FTC shifted its stance on data security, this cannot limit its authority without more."[200]

Some but not all of the issues a V2V Inter-Agency Working Group should address are; the introduction of aftermarket devices into the network,[201] monitoring the accuracy of warnings including new warnings/features as they are added to the V2V system, further restrict access to data by encrypting the Basic Safety Messages transmitted through the network, actively monitor the addition and removal of devices from the Secure Certificate Management System, utilize defensive coding practices in the formulation

---

regulation, said only that such action requires "a reasoned analysis for the change beyond that which may be required when an agency does not act in the first instance.").

[199] *Id. See also Id.* at 502-03 (Scalia explaining "[t]here is, however, no basis…for a requirement that all agency change be subjected to more searching review. Although an agency must ordinarily display awareness that it is changing position…and may sometimes need to account for prior fact finding or certain reliance interests created by a prior policy, it need not demonstrate to a court's satisfaction that the reasons for the new policy are better than the reasons for the old one. It suffices that the new policy is permissible under the statute, that there are good reasons for it, and that the agency believes it to be better, which the conscious change adequately indicates.").

[200] F.T.C. v. Wyndham Worldwide Corp., 10 F.Supp 3d 602, 615 (D.N.J. 2014).

[201] FBI *supra note* 13, (explaining "[t]hird party aftermarket devices with Internet or cellular access plugged into diagnostics ports could also introduce wireless vulnerabilities.").

of basic safety messages, and not allow access by private companies, including use of third party applications, to the DSRC 5.9GHz bandwidth. The Working Group should also consider logging all basic safety messages for auditing purposes.

The DSRC mandate presents an opportunity to begin interagency collaboration in the present rather than suffer through an inevitable jurisdictional tug of war that would result in duplicative, confusing regulations. However, the security and privacy of the public is paramount. If collaboration through an Inter-Agency Working Group is deemed unfeasible then the FCC must put consumer privacy and safety first and act alone to regulate DSRC devices. It is their statutorily mandated responsibility and they must begin now before the cars on America's highways are once again "*Unsafe at Any Speed.*"[202]

---

[202] Nader, *supra* note 23.

The Ransomware Assault on the Healthcare Sector

Malcolm Harkins & Anthony M. Freed[*]

PREFACE

While advanced persistent threats and malware continue to plague organizations across multiple industry verticals, it is the threat from ransomware that is still gaining real traction in today's cybersecurity landscape.

The continued evolution of ransomware altered the threat landscape for both organizations and individuals because it is an inexpensive yet very impactful attack method that can be employed in a wide array of attacks, ranging from phishing, drive-by, and watering hole attacks, to targeted attacks that focus on high-value subjects.

The gamechanger with ransomware is the very real threat of data destruction, whereas before, malware may have been used to steal sensitive data that is ostensibly still accessible by the victim. Ransomware goes further than traditional malware by threatening the complete and utter loss of such sensitive data, creating a new level of threat to both individuals and organizations alike—everyone is a target with ransomware.

---

[*] *Malcolm Harkins* is the Cylance Chief Security and Trust Officer. He is responsible for all aspects of information risk and security at Cylance®, as well as public policy and customer outreach to help improve understanding of cyber risks. He spent 23 years with Intel, most recently as its first Chief Security and Privacy Officer.

Anthony M. Freed is the Cylance Director of Industry Relations and was formerly an infosec journalist who authored numerous feature articles, interviews, and investigative reports which have been sourced and cited by dozens of major media outlets.

This article will provide an overview of what ransomware is, describe the rise of ransomware-as-a-service in the criminal underground, and how the move to electronic records has made the healthcare sector a prime target for potentially costly attacks.

INTRODUCTION

The Health Information Technology for Economic and Clinical Health (HITECH) Act of 2009[1] was designed to be a $31 billion, nationwide transformation of personal health information (PHI) into electronic health records (EHRs).[2] Yet, one unintended consequence of the landmark legislation is the historic number of assaults launched by cybercriminals on the healthcare industry since its enactment. As part of the U.S. Government's 2009 economic stimulus package,[3] HITECH established payment incentives to facilitate the healthcare industry's transition from patient data as paper files locked away in doctors' offices, to electronic records stored on the information superhighway, accessible from anywhere in the world.[4]

---

[1] Health Information Technology for Economic and Clinical Health (HITECH) Provisions of American Recovery and Reinvestment Act of 2009 (ARRA), Title XIII, Pub. L. 111-5, 123 Stat. 115 (2009) (codified as amended in scattered sections of 42 U.S.C.).

[2] CONG. BUDGET OFFICE, COST ESTIMATE: AMERICAN RECOVERY & REINVESTMENT ACT OF 2009 (Jan. 26, 2009), at 16–17; *see also* Rob Girling, *The Elusive Promise of Electronic Health Records*, MEDCITYNEWS, (Jan. 20, 2014, 1:00 PM), https://medcitynews.com/2014/01/elusive-promise-electronic-health-records/?rf=1.

[3] American Recovery and Reinvestment Act of 2009 (ARRA), Pub. L. 111-5, 123 Stat. 115 (signed into law on Feb. 17, 2009 by President Obama).

[4] *See* Standards for the Electronic Health Record Technology Incentive

In theory, EHRs would provide patients and their caregivers with a single source in which to house their medical history and timely data on any current treatments. They would eliminate many of the patient care mistakes that occur due to human error, such as illegible handwriting.[5] They would also supply more efficient patient care by giving healthcare administrators easier access to a holistic picture for each patient.

Unfortunately, one of the worst side effects of EHRs has been the movement of personal and critical patient data from paper records that were never very secure to easily accessible digital files. What was intended to create accessibility for the benefit of the patient has resulted in accessibility for the benefit of cybercriminals with nefarious intentions, which can include reselling the information online, holding it ransom for vast sums of money, or committing identity theft for the purpose of obtaining free medical procedures and prescription medications.[6]

With patient data available to hackers on hospital and healthcare provider networks, cyberattacks in the healthcare

---

Program, 42 C.F.R. § 495.2 (2010) (establishing payment incentive programs for hospitals and healthcare providers that can demonstrate "meaningful use" of certified EHR technology); *see also HITECH Act Enforcement Interim Final Rule*, U.S. DEP'T OF HEALTH & HUMAN SERVICES (June 16, 2017), https://www.hhs.gov/hipaa/for-professionals/special-topics/ HITECH-act-enforcement-interim-final-rule/index.html.

[5] Electronic Prescriptions for Controlled Substances, Interim Final Rule with Request for Comment, 75 Fed. Reg. 16236, 16238 (Mar. 31, 2010) (finding that EHRs and electronic prescription applications "may reduce medical errors caused by illegible handwriting")

[6] Deborah R. Farringer, *Send Us the Bitcoin or Patients Will Die: Addressing the Risks of Ransomware Attacks on Hospitals*, 40 SEATTLE U. L. REV. 937, 937–41, 951–58 (2016).

industry have skyrocketed.[7] The growth in ransomware attacks, in particular, has been a scourge on the U.S. healthcare system. The impact has taken multiple forms, including system and operations downtime, as well as patient care disruptions.[8]

I.   WHAT IS RANSOMWARE?

Ransomware is a type of malware that is typically delivered via a phishing email, which is designed to look like a legitimate email received from a trusted sender. The email will contain an attached file, such as a Microsoft Word document, which when opened, will launch a piece of ransomware. The attachment itself may look and act normal, so as to delay the victim from noticing the behind the scenes deployment. Meanwhile, the ransomware will seek out and encrypt critical files on the user's machine, as well as those found on any connected devices.

Once encryption is complete, the ransomware will display an image on-screen with instructions for how the victim can remit a ransom to obtain a decryption code.[9] This ransom is typically paid in bitcoins, which provides the malware author with an untraceable form of instant

---

[7] U.S. GOV'T INTERAGENCY GUIDANCE DOCUMENT, HOW TO PROTECT YOUR NETWORKS FROM RANSOMWARE, https://www.justice.gov/criminal-ccips/file/872771/download; *see also* Khizar A. Sheikh, *Ransomware, Social Engineering and Organization Liability*, N.J. LAW., Dec. 2016, at 34 (2016).

[8] Farringer, *supra* note 6, at 951–54.

[9] *Id.* at 937–41 ("On the morning of March 28, 2016 . . . a nonprofit hospital system with ten hospitals in Maryland and Washington D.C. were greeted with a pop-up message stating: 'You have 10 days to send us the Bitcoin. . . . [A]fter 10 days we will remove your private key and it's [sic] impossible to recover your files.").

payment.[10]

A. Ransomware-as-a-Service

While some ransomware attacks may be launched by highly skilled programmers with a portfolio of successful attacks, thanks to the proliferation of ransomware-as-a-service (RaaS), novice cybercriminals are often finding success now as well. To expand their reach and operations, ransomware specialists offer their code and expertise to novice hackers online for a nominal fee, for no fee at all, or with a cut of any ransom obtained.

RaaS is quickly becoming one of the most popular forms of cyberextortion. It has been around for many years, but lately there has been a significant increase in the number of variations of the ransomware employed. Due to its notoriety and potential for a high payout, ransomware is quickly evolving, and cybercriminals are developing new ways to distribute malware to make money.

In years past, expert malware authors would package up their know-how into costly exploit kits and sell them on the underground market. Cybercriminals would pay a hefty upfront cost before ever infecting a victim's machine and realizing a profit. One such RaaS is known as Satan Ransomware (Satan).[11]

Satan's developers have posted the ransomware online, making it available for free to the public. Any would-be cybercriminal with absolutely no programming skills can download and deploy *Satan* in just three easy steps, while

---

[10] *Id.* (demanding a ransom of 45 bitcoin, which was equivalent to approximately $19,000).
[11] *Threat Spotlight: Satan RaaS*, CYLANCE (Feb. 6, 2017), https://www.cylance.com/threat-spotlight-satan-raas.

also managing their ransomware campaigns in a central console hosted on the *Satan* developer page. Instructions on payload delivery, translation services, and customer support are even provided to would-be cybercriminals. Then, when *Satan* is successful in an attack, the downloader pays the developer 30% of the ransom obtained, while pocketing the rest.

These are examples from just one industry vertical and three ransomware variants, but they provide real-world lessons on how enterprises can be easily infected, causing great harm to operations, brand reputation, customer relationships, and even the critical infrastructure that organizations all over the world rely upon. The true tragedy of the consequences of ransomware is that they are completely and wholly avoidable with the right endpoint security product.

II.   WHY TARGET THE HEALTHCARE SECTOR WITH RANSOMWARE?

The typical healthcare environment forms a perfect storm when considering the vulnerabilities that attract ransomware attacks: the value of personal health information (PHI). The goal of a healthcare ransomware attack is often either to hold prized PHI hostage in the hopes of receiving payment, or to sell the information to third parties.[12]

Today, PHI data is more valuable on the black market than personal information from financial institutions. In some industries, the ability to access data from prior system backups is sufficient to return the business to an acceptable state of operational effectiveness. However, the

---

[12] *See* Farringer, *supra* note 6, at 951–58.

fluid nature of healthcare settings requires the immediate and dependable availability of real-time data. Backups even a few minutes old can put patients at risk.

PHI is also valuable to cybercriminals in creating a market for multiple secondary transactions. As published by the FBI Cyber Division, cybercriminals sell personal health information on the black market at a rate of $50 for each partial electronic health record, compared to $1 for a stolen social security number or credit card number.[13]

The Lack of Preparation

There is a quote that circulates frequently amongst enterprise workers: "A lack of planning on your part does not constitute an emergency on my part." In the case of healthcare cybersecurity prevention, nothing could be further from the truth. The industry's lack of focus on cybersecurity prevention, and the resulting emergencies, are well documented by both the media and HHS.[14]

A 2015 study conducted by ABI Research states that the healthcare sector is ill prepared for the new cyberage. Hospitals, clinics, trusts, and insurers are constantly under attack from malicious online agents. Medical identity theft and fraud are on the rise, and healthcare providers are struggling to cope, with the past few years seeing hundreds of instances of data breaches leaking millions of personal

---

[13] FED. BUREAU OF INVESTIGATION, HEALTH CARE SYS. & MED. DEVICES AT RISK FOR INCREASED CYBER INTRUSIONS FOR FIN. GAIN (2014), http://www.illuminweb.com/wp-content/uploads/ill-mo-uploads/103/2418/health-systems-cyber-intrusions.pdf.
[14] *See* U.S. DEP'T OF HEALTH & HUMAN SERVS., FACT SHEET: RANSOMWARE & HIPAA, (July 11, 2016), http://www.hhs.gov/sites/default/files/RansomwareFactSheet.pdf; *see also* Farringer, *supra* note 6, at 941–51.

records. And yet the industry spends very little on cybersecurity, in comparison to other regulated critical industries.

ABI Research calculates cybersecurity spending for U.S. healthcare protection will only reach $10 billion globally by 2020, just shy of 10% of total spending on critical infrastructure security.[15] Examples of these gaps in cybersecurity risk management include the continuing presence of deceptive phishing emails and fake website URLs, which can entice employees to unknowingly disclose login information or download malware. Additionally, without the appropriate patches, servers can be vulnerable to threats. Without proper protection, medical devices and industrial control networks can also be accessed, with potential impacts to life-saving systems.

The Lack of Security Awareness Training

A 2015 survey conducted by the Healthcare Information and Management Systems Society revealed that 64% of 297 respondents—each with some responsibility for information security—had experienced a security incident within their healthcare organization caused by phishing.[16] Healthcare professionals, while highly specialized in their clinical disciplines, are generally not well trained in security awareness. The report indicates that otherwise savvy people click on links found in phishing emails due to sophisticated impersonation techniques.

---

[15] ABI RESEARCH, *Healthcare Cybersecurity a Massive Concern as Spending Set to Reach Only US $10 Billion by 2020* (Feb. 25, 2015), https://www.abiresearch.com/press/healthcare-cybersecurity-a-massive-concern-as-spen.

[16] HEALTHCARE INFO. AND MGMT. SYS. SOC'Y, HIMSS CYBERSECURITY SURVEY (2015).

For instance, a healthcare phishing attack might involve an email that looks as if it's coming from a familiar vendor such as LabCorp, with the subject of 'Patient Results Available.' The email will look exactly like a LabCorp email. But the link found in the email will take the recipient to a perfectly "spoofed," identical copy of the login page from LabCorp.com. When the recipient tries to log in, his or her credentials will be stolen. Now, the hacker can log into LabCorp and access PHI directly from the healthcare organization's patient rolls.

Impact on the Medical Industry

There is certainly no shortage of threats to write about these days when it comes to ransomware, and the recent surge of activity involving high profile attacks and their victims. It is deeply concerning to hear about the high-profile medical entities that have been targeted as of lately. In this scenario, the price paid for the attack is not limited to the money paid as the ransom. A ransomware attack on a health center has proven to cause delays in patient care, which can even lead to a loss of human life.

Large health systems are particularly vulnerable to attacks on less secure parts of their systems, given the siloed nature of the systems and technologies created using software from various independently managed vendors. A number of high-profiled ransomware attacks on hospitals have resulted in some of the victims paying out tens of thousands of dollars in ransom money to cybercriminals. Consequently, such payouts have led to multiple new attacks on these very same organizations, and the success of these attacks has emboldened the cybercriminal community as a whole.

Ransomware attacks can lead to dramatic losses for

hospitals, healthcare providers, and other healthcare-based enterprises, including:

Financial:
- Amount of the ransom, if paid
- Regulatory investigations, security audits, fines
- Breach notifications
- Civil litigation and reparations to impacted patients
- System upgrades and restoration
- Revenue Loss

Operational:
- System downtime, loss of productivity
- Loss of new patient admittance
- Cancelled procedures and treatment
- Billing and reimbursement delays

In a highly publicized example of such an attack, forty hospitals that are part of the U.K.'s National Health Service (NHS) were hit simultaneously by the WannaCry Ransomware.[17] Reports of canceled surgeries, medical appointments, and lab results on hold due to the attack flooded the local news, and the public outcry escalated the incident to the global news stage.

The *WannaCry* infection highlighted the outdated and vulnerable infrastructure and security of the NHS. In the weeks following the attack, the hospital network was slow

---

[17] Ian Sherr, *WannaCry Ransomware: Everything You Need to Know*, CNET (May 19, 2017, 12:29 PM), https://www.cnet.com/news/wannacry-wannacrypt-uiwix-ransomware-everything-you-need-to-know.

to recover and restore functions back to each of the forty affected hospitals.

WannaCry: Anatomy of a Ransomware Attack

WannaCry leveraged the *EternalBlue vulnerability,* which took over the news in May 2017 as a result of its inclusion in data leaked by the criminal syndicate known as The Shadow Brokers—a hacking group that has published several leaks of sensitive hacking tools originally developed by the National Security Agency (NSA).[18] Utilized in multiple attacks alongside the also-released *DoublePulsar* exploit, and the cryptocurrency miner malware *Adylkuzz,* these exploits represent just the tip of the cyberwarfare tools that The Shadow Brokers claim to have in their arsenal.[19]

The latest *EternalBlue* and *DoublePulsar* based attacks, delivering the *WannaCry Ransomware,* have been extremely damaging to healthcare organizations, while also impacting over 200,000 endpoints in 150 countries.[20] *WannaCry-WanaCryptor 2.0* was coupled with the *EternalBlue* exploit, allowing it to automatically propagate itself to vulnerable machines across the Internet. While not technically advanced, the use of *EternalBlue* and *DoublePulsar* created a ransomworm that spread much faster than any other previously reported ransomware

---

[18] *Id.*

[19] *Threat Spotlight: The Shadow Brokers and EternalPulsar Malware,* CYLANCE (Aug. 15, 2017), https://www.cylance.com/en_us/blog/threat-spotlight-the-shadow-brokers-and-eternalpulsar-malware.html

[20] Rohit Langde, *WannaCry Ransomware: A Detailed Analysis of the Attack,* TECHSPECTIVE (Sept. 26, 2017), https://techspective.net/2017/09/26/wannacry-ransomware-detailed-analysis-attack.

outbreak.

This attack exploits a flaw in the *Server Message Block (SMB)* in Microsoft Windows, which can allow for remote code execution upon proper and successful exploitation. The flaw was patched in Microsoft's March 2017 update cycle (MS17-10).[21] However, many network environments are still behind on these patches and for various reasons—such as computers running on legacy operating systems like Windows XP, which are no longer updated/supported with security patches, leaving their systems entirely exposed and vulnerable to attack.[22]

Leveraging this exploit, the attackers can fully execute arbitrary code. In the case of the *WanaCrypt* issue, we are dealing with a ransomware executable that includes additional worm functionality. It has the ability to scan and locate other machines, and propagate itself to other adjacent and exposed hosts via the *EternalBlue* vulnerability. Due to the nature of the flaw, machines that are propagated via the worm functionality do not require interaction from the user on the victimized host.

The worm/ransomware binary handles the remote execution. In most confirmable cases today, stage one is a malicious phishing email. This includes an attachment that the victim executes, which infects them, while simultaneously kickstarting stage two—the worm-type functionality and internal propagation/pivoting.

Ransomware has been around for well over a decade, but traditional antivirus solutions still require every single

---

[21] MICROSOFT, SEC. UPDATE FOR MICROSOFT WINDOWS SMB SERVER (4013389) (Mar. 14, 2017), https://docs.microsoft.com/en-us/security-updates/securitybulletins/2017/ms17-010.

[22] Farringer, *supra* note 6, at 957 (noting critics see an industry-wide culture that is unwilling to adapt to, and more importantly invest in, the advancing technological landscape).

piece of malware to be discovered by its execution on an endpoint, meaning that these solutions cannot stop ransomware until it infects its first victim. If your organization is the "sacrificial lamb" that traditional antivirus providers need, you could be faced with an extremely costly ransom, which may or may not yield the ability to decrypt your locked data.

The Sense of Urgency

The obligation of healthcare organizations to maintain the integrity of patient care environments and the accuracy of medical records is a powerful incentive to return the environment to its original state. But this sense of urgency held by healthcare providers to return to normal operations as quickly as possible also provides a strong advantage to the perpetrators of ransomware attacks.[23]

When hospitals lose control of their data, they risk being in violation of HIPAA regulations as outlined in the HIPAA Breach Notification Rule.[24] The rule requires HIPAA-covered entities and associates to provide notification following a breach of unsecured PHI. Older and less sophisticated strains of malware wrap or encrypt the PHI data, never moving it from the server or desktop environment. A party who does not have the proper authorization cannot view it. A current list of a list of breaches of unsecured protected health information affecting 500 or more individuals is available.[25]

However, more sophisticated malware variants are

---

[23] *Id.* at 951–58.

[24] HIPAA Breach Notification Rule, 45 C.F.R. §§ 164.400–414 (2009).

[25] U.S. DEP'T OF HEALTH & HUMAN SERV., BREACH PORTAL: NOTICE TO THE SEC'Y OF HHS BREACH OF UNSECURED PROTECTED HEALTH INFO. (2018), https://ocrportal.hhs.gov/ocr/breach/breach_report.jsf.

able to access the data, and some sit dormant for long periods of time before creating the breach. In such a case, the burden of proof is on each healthcare organization to have solutions in place that can clearly determine whether or not the ransomware viewed or accessed any PHI data, potentially enabling the ransomware author to download or view it.

III.   CONCLUSION – AN OUNCE OF PREVENTION

In February 2016, the Ponemon Institute released the results of its 2016 State of Cybersecurity in Healthcare Organizations study.[26] According to its researchers:

- Healthcare organizations average one cyberattack per month;
- 48% of respondents stated that their organizations have experienced a security breach involving the loss or exposure of patient information data in the last 12 months; and
- Only half of the respondents indicated that their organization has an incident response plan in place.

With findings like this, the answer seems obvious. Benjamin Franklin said, "[b]y failing to prepare, you are preparing to fail." With the current opportunity for healthcare decision makers to hardwire their enterprises with next-generation endpoint protection solutions, the industry could potentially begin to see reports of cyberattacks drop significantly within the coming twelve months.

---

[26] PONEMON INST., THE STATE OF CYBERSECURITY IN HEALTHCARE ORGS. IN 2016 (Feb. 2016), https://cdn2.esetstatic.com/eset/US/resources/docs/white-papers/State_of_Healthcare_Cybersecurity_Study.pdf.

The responsibility to take appropriate steps toward the right solution now lies is in the hands of board members, C-level executives, and IT security specialists. In parallel, employees must be trained to identify phishing events, and to address them in a way that reduces security risk.

Cyberattacks are planned and delivered in nearly the same manner, seldom straying from a high-level process map known as the Cyber Kill Chain. The only variable is the amount of technical or personal resources cybercriminals spend on the different stages of an attack. No matter where your current internal infrastructure lies on the spectrum of cybersecurity preparedness, understand that there are emerging next-generation solutions available that can stop malicious files before they ever execute, with no "sacrificial lamb" required.

The problem with legacy security solutions is that adversaries can continually evolve their techniques and tactics to bypass them, leaving enterprises vulnerable to attacks. This means that traditional solutions are reactive in nature and rely on a constant stream of "signature updates" to tell them what type of files to look for after an attack was successful on some other system, known as "zero-day" attacks. Traditional security solutions are built around a basic set of rules and signature files that are costly and high risk because they require many "sacrificial lambs" before they can create the ability to block an attack—meaning it is not possible to identify a new threat until after some damage is done. This is what is occurring in the health care industry, as well as in other sectors. It is time for us to innovate and take action faster than we currently have. We need to implement new security architectures that will provide significant improvement in our ability to mitigate and manage our growing information risks.

Any future security architecture to be implemented

must provide for better prevention, and it also must be more flexible, dynamic, and more granular than traditional security models. A new architecture also needs to greatly improve threat management. We need to do this in the upfront design, development, and validation during the creation of technology to reduce vulnerabilities well before the technology gets deployed. And as new attacks appear, we need a security system that is able to recognize the good from the bad in milliseconds, so that it can stop the bad and allow the good. For any attack that gets past these preventive controls, we need to be able to learn as much as we possibly can without compromising the user's computing performance or privacy. This information enables us to investigate exactly what occurred, so we can take immediate action to mitigate the risk, whilst also learning how to prevent similar attacks in the future.

A control architecture should assume that attempts at compromise are inevitable—but we should also understand that it is possible to achieve real prevention for 99% or more of the risks that could occur, including that of malicious code and zero-day attacks caused by mutated malware. Should a piece of malicious code attempt to execute, we can then instantly apply artificial intelligence and machine learning to analyze the features of files, executables, and binaries to stop the code dead in its tracks, before it ever has a chance to harm the environment. For the remaining attacks— representing less than 1% of malware—we need to focus heavily on survivability.

JFK once said: "The problems of the world cannot be solved by skeptics or cynics whose horizons are limited by the obvious realities. We need men who can dream of things that never were and ask why not." When we innovate and implement a new security architecture focused on prevention of risk at the core, coupled with AI based detection and response, we can achieve a dramatic reduction in risk and an equally dramatic improvement in our health care system.

German IT Security Law
John A. Foulks[*]

This country brief is meant to give the reader an overview of the history and present status of IT security regulation in Germany. It follows a chronological organization, covering the period from 1991 through the end of 2017. The German federal parliament, the Bundestag, began updating and expanding the mandate of the Federal Office for Information Security (the *Bundesamt für Sicherheit in der Informationstechnik* – the "BSI") in 2015. Generally, the aim has been to secure critical infrastructure, defined in terms of public access to a list of basic services and necessities, from vulnerabilities due to the ubiquitous use of information technology. The European legislation behind the most recent set of German enactments is introduced in turn. The presentation finishes by identifying a foreseeable European-level regulation of cybersecurity product certification for the single European market, as well as the establishment of the European Union Agency for Network and Information Security ("ENISA") as the pan-European cybersecurity agency. The article may serve as an introduction and a starting point for more in-depth research. It identifies and summarizes major substantive provisions of the respective enactments and regulations over time. It also

---

[*] *John A. Foulks* is an alumnus of Dartmouth College, Indiana University and, since 2017, Rutgers Law School. Through Rutgers, he attended the international exchange program at Bucerius Law School in Hamburg in 2016. He joined the JLCW editorial staff in 2017. John is currently a Chancery Division law clerk at New Jersey Superior Court and is admitted to practice in New Jersey. He has been living in Germany or working with German in one way or another nearly nonstop since 1994, including studying, teaching, and translating.

offers assorted insights into the legislative history. The subject matter is presented in abridged form. In general, it was necessary to dispense with many details, in particular when it came to minute legislative tweaks to existing law in several areas in order to accommodate new cybersecurity regulations.

I.   CREATION OF THE FEDERAL OFFICE FOR INFORMATION
      SECURITY (THE BSI)

The BSI, a subordinate agency within the Federal Ministry of the Interior (*Bundesministerium des Inneren* – the "BMI"), is Germany's national cybersecurity authority. It is tasked with "shap[ing] information security in digitization through prevention, detection and reaction for government, business and society."[1] The BSI was established almost three decades ago, by way of legislation that took effect in 1991.[2] The legislation that called the BSI into existence defined "information technology" as any technological means of distributing or transferring information, and "security" as the observance of standards to ensure the availability, integrity or confidentiality of information. The means of achieving security were to be found within IT systems and components, and in the ways such systems and components were used.[3] At the time, the

---

[1] *Das BSI*, BUNDESAMT FÜR SICHERHEIT IN DER INFORMATIONSTECHNIK, http://www.bsi.bund.de/DE/DasBSI/Gesetz/gesetz_node.html (last visited Mar. 5, 2018) (Ger.).

[2] Gesetz über die Errichtung des Bundesamtes für Sicherheit in der Informationstechnik [BSI-Errichtungsgesetz] [BSI Formation Act], Dec. 17, 1990, BGBL I at 2834, as amended by Art. 11 of the Verordnung [V] [Regulation] of Nov. 25, 2003, BGBL I at 2304 (Ger.).

[3] *See id.* § 2.

Bundestag charged the new BSI with investigating security risks associated with the use of IT and developing preventive measures, in the form of security processes and devices. The BSI was also charged with developing criteria, processes, and tools for testing and evaluating the security of IT systems and components, and carrying out that testing and evaluation.[4]

With certain exceptions, the 1991 law expressly limited the scope of the BSI's activity to securing the IT-related applications of the German federal government.[5] It could, however, provide security advice to manufacturers, merchants and users of IT, in particular regarding the risks associated with using such IT equipment.[6] By way of background to the most recent developments (through 2017), it bears emphasis that the 1991 Act provided that manufacturers and merchants of IT systems should be able to apply to the BSI for certification of their products.

The BSI was empowered to grant IT product security certification on two broad conditions. The first was that systems and components should fulfill generally recognized criteria, or criteria established by the BSI. The second condition was that the BMI (the BSI's parent agency) had to determine that no federal security or preponderating public interests weighed against certification.[7] Security certificates from other "recognized" agencies in the European Community were to be recognized by the BSI if such certificates demonstrated an "equivalent security" level.[8] As of the end of 2017, the member-state-specific product certification regimes now in place let product cybersecurity

---

[4] *See id.* § 3(1) nos. 1 – 3.
[5] *See id.* § 1(1) no. 1; §§ 4 – 6.
[6] *See id.* § 3(1) no. 7.
[7] *See id.* § 4.
[8] *See id.* § 4(4).

certifications be recognized across member states pursuant to a small number of multilateral agreements among subsets of EU member states.[9] These appear likely to be displaced or preempted in the foreseeable future as the European Commission has issued a proposed regulation on the topic.[10]

II.   MAJOR OVERHAUL OF THE BSI STATUTE IN 2009

In 2009, the Bundestag passed very significant amendments by way of an act styled as one "to increase the security of the IT of the federal government."[11] The act (hereinafter "the BSIG of 2009") expanded the set of defined terms to refer to "communications technology operated by federal authorities as well as its interfaces,"[12] with "interfaces" further defined according to the official English translation[13] as "security-relevant gateways within federal communications technology and between this technology and the information technology of individual federal

---

[9] *Commission Proposal for a Regulation of the European Parliament and of the Council on ENISA, the "EU Cybersecurity Agency," and repealing Regulation (EU) 526/2013, and on Information and Communication Technology cybersecurity certification ("Cybersecurity Act")*, at 1, COM (2017) 477 final (Sept. 13, 2017), https://ec.europa.eu/info/law/better-regulation/initiatives/com-2017-477_en.

[10] *Id.*

[11] Gesetz zur Stärkung der Sicherheit in der Informationstechnik des Bundes [BSIG] [Act on the Federal Office for Information Security], Aug. 14, 2009, BGBL I, 54, at 2821-26, *translation at* https://www.gesetze-im-internet.de/englisch_bsig/index.html (Ger.) [hereinafter BSIG of 2009]. As of February 2018, the cited English translation does not reflect substantial subsequent amendments; however, the German text at the same location does. See the amending acts cited below at notes 31 & 65.

[12] *Id.* § 2(4).

[13] *See* BSIG of 2009, *supra* note 11.

authorities, groups of federal authorities, or third parties."[14] New definitions also included harmful software, security gaps or flaws, protocol data and data transmissions.[15] Only a selection is cited here. The amended definitions alone indicate the expanded scope of the law precipitated by the 2009 amendments.

The tasks delegated to the BSI multiplied accordingly. The BSI was now responsible for defending against threats as well as collecting and analyzing information about security risks and measures.[16] Further, it was tasked with operating cryptographic and security management systems for other agencies of the federal government, and with testing and advising on these systems.[17] The BSI retained its former advisory role but was now also charged with issuing warnings to German federal and state entities, private manufacturers, merchants and users of IT concerning the security thereof.[18] Furthermore, the BSI was charged with establishing suitable communication channels for purposes of timely recognizing, reacting to, and overcoming crises affecting critical *information* infrastructure.[19]

The BSI's reach and responsibility was thus limited because of the way the Bundestag had defined its mission. Instead of mandating that the BSI safeguard critical

---

[14] BSIG of 2009, *supra* note 11, § 2(3), (4), at 2821. Note the carve-outs for IT operated by the other constitutional organs, namely the two federal legislative houses, *Bundestag* [federal parliament] and *Bundesrat* [federal council], the *Bundesrechnungshof* [the independent federal auditing agency] and the federal courts.

[15] *Id.*

[16] *Id.* § 3(1) no. 2.

[17] *Id.* § 3(1) nos. 8, 9, at 2822.

[18] BSIG of 2009, *supra* note 11, § 3(1) no. 14, at 2822.

[19] *Id.* § 3(1) no. 15, at 2822 (emphasis added).

infrastructure, presuming (as we must) that IT produces a new set of vulnerabilities anywhere it is used, the Bundestag at the time tasked the BSI with reacting to and overcoming crises affecting critical *information infrastructure* only. The good to be protected was thus conceived of narrowly. But it has since become obvious that infrastructure in general has been made to depend on computerized information, and it is no longer possible to observe the ubiquity and scale of information and be content to secure only *its* infrastructure. Subsequent amendments have addressed the formerly inadequate scheme. Whether they have done so well has been the subject of debate both within the Bundestag, as well as between it and the government, in advance of the subsequent amendments discussed below.

Still, the associated principles of cybersecurity survived the subsequent paradigm shift. The 2009 overhaul of the BSI's mandate called for the agency to coordinate a cooperative effort with private industry, albeit with the express, relatively narrow aim of protecting the good referred to in limited fashion as critical information infrastructure.[20] The BSIG of 2009 overall not only greatly expanded the role of the BSI at the time but also still embodies the primary crystallization of the current approach. Section 4 of the BSIG of 2009 established the BSI as the "central clearinghouse"[21] for cooperation among German federal agencies on IT security. The BSI was tasked with observing and evaluating attacks against IT systems and informing federal agencies of attacks.[22] Reciprocally, the new law obligated other federal agencies to communicate

---

[20] *Id.*

[21] *Id.* § 4, at 2822. Again note that the English translation published as of this writing does not reflect substantial further amendments enacted in 2015 and 2017.

[22] *Id.* § 4(2).

relevant information to the BSI should it come to the other agencies' attention first.[23] The BSI was also empowered to assist the German states, upon their request, with securing their own IT.[24]

The BSIG imposed certain limits on the BSI's activities were also imposed, and these have also survived subsequent amendments. It has been a source of continual controversy that individually identifiable data collected by the BSI acting under its cyber security mandate could be available to various other security or law enforcement agencies. The limits imposed on the BSI therefore involve administrative and judicial oversight around data protection issues.

For one thing, the 2009 amendments expressly preserved the norms otherwise applicable to handling personally identifiable information.[25] In operating federal communications technology, and at the "interfaces" of such technology as defined above,[26] communications protocol data would foreseeably accumulate. Whether and how such data was permitted to be automatically analyzed or retained was made to depend upon a series of conditions. If communication protocol data contained personally identifiable information or data that was subject to the norms governing secrecy in telecommunications, then the extent of automated analysis was limited to what was required to recognize, isolate and eliminate disturbances, and to defend against malicious software.[27] The generally permitted automated analysis just described had to occur right away; and such data could not be retained at all after the stated

---

[23] *Id.* § 4(3).
[24] *Id.* § 3(2), at 2822.
[25] BSIG of 2009, *supra* note 11, § 4(5), at 2823.
[26] *Id.* § 2(4).
[27] *Id.* § 5(1).

objective had been accomplished.[28] Non-automated use of the data, or use in a way that would associate it with particular persons, was permissible only under a further series of detailed restrictions. Not automated use of the data had to be supported by a reasonable suspicion arising from particularized facts. Moreover, the scope of the authority to analyze such data was limited to what was required to confirm or allay suspicion of, and to defend against, malicious software.[29] Affected persons had to be informed of non-automated analysis of the data. Rights related to data protection and core personal privacy interests were to be respected unless the government could satisfy a number of conditions all involving oversight by federal agents charged with data protection, or by the courts.[30]

III.   THE 2015 AMENDMENTS TO THE BSIG

The BSIG received its next major overhaul just roughly six years later on July 17, 2015.[31] According to the BSI, the 2015 enactment expanded the agency's role with the aim of bolstering IT security of critical infrastructure beyond the administrative boundaries of the federal government.[32] The legislative materials state that the basic motivation for the enactment was to better protect the authenticity, availability, confidentiality and integrity of IT systems for businesses, citizens' online activity, and the BSI and *Bundeskriminalamt* (the Federal Criminal Police

---

[28] *Id.*

[29] *Id.* § 5(2), 5(3).

[30] *Id.* § 5(4) – (7).

[31] IT-Sicherheitsgesetz [IT Security Act], July 17, 2015, BGBL I, 31, at 1324–31 (Ger.).

[32] BUNDESAMT FÜR SICHERHEIT IN DER INFORMATIONSTECHNIK, *supra* note **Error! Bookmark not defined.**.

Office).[33]

Generally referred to as the IT Security Act, the 2015 amendments appointed the BSI as a threat sharing agency if not in terms, then at least in effect.[34] This follows from the legislative materials: the Bundestag sought to obligate operators of critical infrastructure to adhere to a set of minimum standards for cybersecurity and to notify the BSI in the event of cybersecurity incidents.[35] With the BSI continuously disseminating intelligence gathered from all operators of critical infrastructure, a given operator supposedly would reap more in return than it had provided, in the form of better information and know-how about threats.[36] The Bundesrat's position document asserts that the IT Security Act observed the basic principle behind the European Commission's then-proposal, enacted later by the European Union as the NIS Directive.[37]

The document offering the draft legislation[38] sought

---

[33] *See, e.g.*, Gesetzentwurf der Bundesregierung [Cabinet draft], Entwurf eines Gesetzes zur Erhöhung der Sicherheit informationstechnischer Systeme (IT-Sicherheitsgesetz) [Draft of an Act to Increase the Security of IT Systems – IT Security Act], Dec. 29, 2014, BUNDESRAT DRUCKSACHEN [BR] 643/14 at 2, https://www.bundesrat.de/SharedDocs/drucksachen/2014/0601-0700/643-14.pdf (Ger.) [hereinafter BR 643/14]; *see also* Gesetzentwurf der Bundesregierung [Cabinet draft], Entwurf eines Gesetzes zur Erhöhung der Sicherheit informationstechnischer Systeme (IT-Sicherheitsgesetz) [Draft of an act to increase the security of IT systems – IT Security Act], DEUTSCHER BUNDESTAG: DRUCKSACHEN [BT] 18/4096 at 19, http://dip21.bundestag.de/dip21/btd/18/040/1804096.pdf (Ger.) [hereinafter BT 18/4096].
[34] *See id.*
[35] *Id.*
[36] *Id.*
[37] BR 643/14, *supra* note 33, at 3.
[38] BT 18/4096, *supra* note 33.

to recognize that telecommunications providers are one key to cybersecurity. They would be obligated to maintain state of the art IT security in order to meet the legal standards for telecommunications secrecy as well as to secure personally identifiable information and the availability of their own services. The Bundesnetzagentur (Federal Network Agency), otherwise charged with overseeing telecommunications markets,[39] would handle law enforcement aspects as well as the obligatory notification of the BSI in the event of cyber incidents. The verbal standard "state of the art" has been controversial, as discussed below.

The IT Security Act's provisions were detailed and numerous.[40] Significantly, this legislation amended the phrase "critical information infrastructure" in section 3(1), second sentence, no. 15 of the BSIG, the limiting phrase which was a legacy of the BSIG of 2009.[41] The operative phrase is now "security in the IT of *critical* infrastructures."[42]

An amendment to section 3 of the Act carried out the legislative purpose of having the BSI function as a threat sharing agency by permitting the sharing of intelligence with third parties.[43] Legislative materials elaborate that this

---

[39] *Functions,* BUNDESNETZAGENTUR, https://www.bundesnetzagentur.de/EN/General/Bundesnetzagentur/Ab out/Functions/functions_node.html (last visited Dec. 16, 2017).
[40] A reader already familiar with the provisions might find fault with the priorities of the present selection. Moreover, one should not be tempted to conclude that a particular specific subject matter is left unregulated by the within law simply because it is not highlighted here.
[41] See *supra* note 19 and the accompanying discussion there.
[42] *Compare* the BSIG of 2009, *supra* note 11, *with* the IT Security Act *supra* note 31, no. 3.a)bb), at 1324. See also the associated discussion supra at note
[43] *Das BSI,* BUNDESAMT FÜR SICHERHEIT IN DER INFORMATIONSTECHNIK,

provision was intended to extend not only to any other operator of critical infrastructure but to a very broad set of organizational types. Namely, threat intelligence could be shared with

> other facilities or businesses which, though not operators of critical infrastructure in terms of the BSIG, are nonetheless known to be part of Critical Infrastructure in the broader sense, or which otherwise have a justified security interest in the information in question (for example in the culture and media sector, which is not covered, or research organizations).[44]

Moreover, the BSI was made the central agency for IT security cooperation with competent agencies abroad, without prejudice to the competences of other German federal agencies.[45]

During the legislative process in 2015, the Bundesrat (the Federal Council) criticized certain terms in the proposed Act as too indefinite. In response, the government cited constitutional case law upholding the use of indefinite terms as unavoidable in light of many multifaceted, real-world circumstances.[46] The very dynamic nature of the cybersecurity field, argued the law's sponsors, meant concrete future developments could not be accounted for. Indeterminate legal terms were therefore supposed to preserve the relevance of the statute over time and make it

---

http://www.bsi.bund.de/DE/DasBSI/Gesetz/gesetz_node.html (last visited Mar. 5, 2018) (Ger.); BR 643/14, *supra* note 33, at 29.

[44] BR 643/14, *supra* note 33, at 29 (translation by the author).

[45] IT Security Act, *supra* note 31, no. 3.a)cc), at 1324.

[46] BT 18/4906, *supra* note 33, at 48 (Ger.) (internal citations to constitutional case law omitted).

tech-agnostic.[47]

The definition selected for "critical infrastructure" extended to facilities and installations or components thereof that were highly meaningful for the functioning of society because their failure or impairment would lead to severe shortages or endanger public safety.[48] The Act designated a list of critical sectors as critical in terms of securing the basic needs of citizens. These were the energy, IT and telecom, logistics and transportation, healthcare, water, food, and finance and insurance sectors.[49] Due to the complexity of determining what entities were subject to the Act, authority was delegated to the BSI to issue further regulations of critical infrastructures on the basis of ongoing consultations with affected persons, entities and experts.[50] (These regulations are addressed briefly below.)

The Bundestag also recognized that there was additional infrastructure qualitatively just as critical as what the Act addressed expressly. But the competence to regulate these other categories was not among its constitutionally enumerated powers. State and municipal governments, as well as entities in the culture and media sector, are examples of those that are left to German state law.[51] Federal government infrastructure belonging to the executive and legislative branches, on the other hand, does fall within the scope of the Act.[52]

The BSI's authorization to issue warnings was modified. The agency could now issue warnings either directly to the general public or only to those affected. It

---

[47] *Id.*

[48] IT Security Act, *supra* note 31, no. 2, at 1324.

[49] *Id.* no. 2.1.

[50] *Id.* no. 2.2; *see also* BT 18/4096, *supra* note 33 at 29.

[51] BT 18/4096, *supra* note 33 at 29.

[52] *Id.*

could warn of security flaws in IT products and services, malicious software, or loss of or unauthorized access to data. The BSI was permitted to bring in third parties where an effective and timely warning required it.[53] But most salient in the BSI's own view were new provisions requiring operators of critical infrastructure to demonstrate regularly, or at least every two years, that they are practicing state-of-the-art IT security. Paramount in the agency's view was also the authority to order remediation of deficiencies in conjunction with other regulators.[54] Operators were obligated to notify the BSI of any serious problems with their IT if the potential existed that critical services would be affected.[55] Regulated entities had six months to provide the BSI with a continuously available point of contact.[56]

This overview of the substance of the 2015 IT Security Act concludes by summarizing the parliamentary opposition's criticism of the legislation as enacted.[57] This is informative as to the realm of possibility—or at least as to the range of public sentiment at the time—beyond what the parliamentary majority eventually resolved to enact.

The oppositional parties proposed a resolution referring to Edward Snowden by name and recognizing a cybersecurity threat from state agencies, in particular Western intelligence agencies.[58] The view was that any

---

[53] IT Security Act, *supra* note 31, no. 5, at 1325.
[54] BUNDESAMT FÜR SICHERHEIT IN DER INFORMATIONSTECHNIK, *supra* note **Error! Bookmark not defined.**.
[55] *Id.*; *see also* IT Security Act, *supra* note 31, at 1325-27.
[56] *Id.* at 1326.
[57] *See* Beschlussempfehlung und Bericht des Innenausschusses [Recommendation for resolution and report of the interior committee], June 6, 2015, BT 18/5121, 12-14, 17-18, http://dip21.bundestag.de/dip21/btd/18/051/1805121.pdf (Ger.).
[58] *Id.* at 12.

legislation ought to protect against violations of the citizens' fundamental right to confidentiality, as well as support the integrity of IT systems they use.[59] The new law ought to have contained additional provisions, it thought. Specifically, it should have paid more attention to proportionality in determining when personally identifiable information was permitted to be processed. The standard triggering cybersecurity incident reporting should have been stated more broadly than "serious disturbances." Mass data retention solely for the purpose of IT security should have been proscribed. Industrial competition around good IT security should have been better incentivized. Penetration testing for government and private IT systems ought to have been implemented. "State of the art" cybersecurity should have expressly included risk analysis. Sanctions for failure to follow security standards ought to have been more effective. Legal liability, *e.g.*, for negligent implementation of IT or failure to eliminate security flaws, ought to have been imposed. Immediate publication of threat data and security flaws coming to the BSI's attention ought to have been mandatory. End-to-end encryption, open-source hardware and software-based infrastructure and bug bounty programs ought to have been made the norm.

Since the foregoing list was not enacted into law, the practitioner is left to determine the relevance of the opposition's demands or the extent to which the law, as enacted, reasonably requires any of the above, though it was not spelled out in a specific provision as enacted.

---

[59] *Id.* at 12.

IV.   THE NIS DIRECTIVE OF THE EUROPEAN UNION

A mere sketch of the NIS Directive[60] appears here as the background to the most recent amendment of the corresponding German statute, discussed hereafter. After the Bundestag passed the IT Security Act of 2015, the European Union issued a directive on the security of network and information systems (the "NIS Directive").[61] The European Parliament adopted the NIS Directive on July 6, 2016, to enter into force in August, 2017.[62] Member states have until May 9, 2018 to transpose the NIS Directive into national law[63] and until November 9, 2018 to identify operators of "essential services."[64] The Bundestag regards "essential services" as the equivalent of "critical infrastructure."[65] The

---

[60] Directive (EU) 2016/1148 of the European Parliament and of the Council of 6 July 2016 Concerning Measures for a High Common Level of Security of Network and Information Systems Across the Union, 2016 O.J. (L 194) 59, 1 – 30, http://eur-lex.europa.eu/legal-content/EN/TXT/PDF/?uri=CELEX:32016L1148&from=EN [hereinafter NIS Directive].

[61] *The Directive on Security of Network and Information Systems (NIS Directive)*, EUROPEAN COMMISSION, https://ec.europa.eu/digital-single-market/en/network-and-information-security-nis-directive (last visited December 10, 2017).

[62] Martin Schallbruch, *NIS-Richtlinie verabschiedet: schwierige Umsetzung für digitale Dienste*, CRONLINE (July 15, 2016, 6:06 a.m.), www.cr-online.de/blog/2016/07/15/nis-richtlinie-verabschiedet-schwierige-umsetzung-fuer-digitale-dienste/ (Ger.).

[63] *Id.*

[64] *Id.*

[65] Gesetzentwurf der Bundesregierung [Cabinet draft], Entwurf eines Gesetzes zur Umsetzung der Richtlinie (EU) 2016/1148 des Europäischen Parlaments und des Rates vom 6. Juli 2016 über Maßnahmen zur Gewährleistung eines hohen gemeinsamen Sicherheitsniveaus von Netz- und Informationssystemen in der Union [Draft of an act to implement Directive (EU) 2016/1148 of the European Parliament and of the Council *etc.*], BT 18/11242, Feb. 20,

NIS Directive leaves it to EU member states to specify what the corresponding services or infrastructure are.

According to the European Commission, the legislation was intended to "boost the overall level of cybersecurity in the EU" by several means.[66] Member states are to establish computer security incident response teams (CSIRTs) as well as a national authority for network and information security, as a preparation for cybersecurity incidents. The NIS Directive envisions both long-term as well as incident-related information sharing and cooperation among member-state representatives, the European Commission and the European Union Agency for Network and Information Security ("ENISA").[67]

"Digital services," defined as online marketplaces, online search engines and cloud computing services, were deemed essential and made subject to the regulation.[68] The EU member state in which such a service maintains its head office shall have jurisdiction. But if a digital service were offered in the EU by a provider without an establishment of that kind, then the provider "shall designate a representative in the Union . . . established in one of those Member States where the services are offered . . . [and] be deemed to be under the jurisdiction of the Member State where the representative is established."[69]

2017, at 1 (Ger.), http://dip21.bundestag.de/dip21/btd/18/112/1811242.pdf.

[66] EUROPEAN COMMISSION, *supra* note 61.

[67] *See* NIS Directive, *supra* note 60, declaration (4), at 2 ("For that group to be effective and inclusive, it is essential that all Member States have minimum capabilities and a strategy ensuring a high level of security of network and information systems in their territory.").

[68] *See supra* note 60, Annex III, at 30.

[69] *See supra* note 60, Chapter V, at 21, 23 (on digital service providers' obligations generally and Art. 18 on member states' jurisdiction specifically).

V.   THE 2017 AMENDMENT TO THE BSIG

Subsequently to the NIS Directive, the Bundestag once more amended the BSIG to transpose the Directive into national law.[70] An EU directive sets mandatory goals or standards the means of achieving which are left up to the national (member-state) legislatures.[71] The proponents of this set of amendments to the BSIG considered that the provisions of the earlier IT Security Act on operators of critical infrastructure[72] in Germany were substantially equivalent to the call of the NIS Directive regarding "essential services"[73] in the EU. However, the parliamentary opposition formally renewed its concern that the verbal standard for mandatory reporting, namely "serious security incidents," left too much wiggle room. It urged that more had to be done to prevent intelligence agencies having any use of data collected under the BSIG.[74] It also renewed its call for heightened liability provisions to force critical infrastructure operators to invest in IT security.[75]   The   legislative

---

[70] Gesetz zur Umsetzung der Richtlinie (EU) 2016/1148 des Europäischen Parlaments und des Rates vom 6. Juli 2016 über Maßnahmen zur Gewährleistung eines hohen gemeinsamen Sicherheitsniveaus von Netz- und Informationssystemen in der Union vom 23. Juni 2017 [An act to give effect to Directive (EU) 2016/1148], BGBL I, 40, 1885 – 1892 (Ger.).

[71] *See Regulations, Directives and Other Acts*, EUROPEAN UNION, https://europa.eu/european-union/eu-law/legal-acts_en (last visited February 20, 2018).

[72] *See* IT Security Act, *supra* note 31, § 2 (10).

[73] Beschlussempfehlung und Bericht des Innenausschusses [Recommendation for resolution and report of the Committee on Internal Affairs], Mar. 30, 2017, BT 18/11808, at 1, http://dipbt.bundestag.de/dip21/btd/18/118/1811808.pdf (Ger.).

[74] *Id.* at 11.

[75] *Id.* at 11-12.

committee that reviewed the cabinet draft prior to adoption of the 2017 amendments drew attention to internet-of-things (hereinafter "IoT") devices, demanding a system of voluntary certification and quality labeling as a way to communicate indirectly with consumers.[76] The committee criticized as insufficient the EU regulations on IoT device security and called upon the German federal government to work out the labeling issues in conjunction with stakeholders and the BSI. It believed the government should lobby the EU to provide mandatory IT security requirements for IoT devices marketed in the EU.[77] Observing that security could not be achieved unless device owners act reasonably, labeling was deemed an appropriate way to let reasonable consumer behavior begin fundamentally with the choice of device.[78]

Despite the criticism, the legislation that was eventually enacted conformed German national law to the NIS Directive. It updated definitions so as to subject digital services offered within the EU to regulation under the BSIG regardless of the operator's presence in the territory.[79] Quantitative thresholds would exempt smaller operators. Certain exceptions applied to online marketplaces depending on the locality where the parties would be deemed

---

[76] *See id.* at 8.

[77] *Id.*

[78] *Id.* at 11.

[79] *See* An act to give effect to Directive (EU) 2016/1148, *supra* note 70 at 1885; Gesetzentwurf der Bundesregierung [cabinet draft], Entwurf eines Gesetzes zur Umsetzung der Richtlinie (EU) 2016/1148 des Europäischen Parlaments und des Rates vom 6. Juli 2016 über Maßnahmen zur Gewährleistung eines hohen gemeinsamen Sicherheitsniveaus von Netz- und Informationssystemen in der Union [Draft of an act to give effect to Directive (EU) 2016/1148], BT 18/11242, Feb. 20, 2017, at 34, http://dip21.bundestag.de/dip21/btd/18/112/1811242.pdf.

to have entered into the contract of sale.[80] "Search engines" for purposes of the regulation were limited to services permitting queries on arbitrary topics.[81] Cloud computing was so defined as to apply to a "broad palette" of computational services—servers, networks, storage, applications or others—that were scalable, elastic, and available to multiple users.[82] The BSI was permitted to provide more comprehensive technical expertise at the request of the German states than had been available under the prior law, which had not authorized assistance beyond law enforcement and state-owned IT.[83] The act also provided for mobile incident response teams (generally "MIRTs") with which the BSI could support other entities in recovering their IT systems in the event of cyberattack.

Several provisions of Chapter II, Annex 1 to the NIS Directive, related to the activity of MIRTs, are implemented through the insertion of a new section 5a of the BSIG. They provide that MIRTs may assist federal government agencies, operators of critical infrastructure generally, and others in exceptional circumstances. Some measures were supposed to make it more palatable for a private firm to engage a MIRT with respect to cost or the risk of incurring telecommunications secrecy violations.[84] Provisions related to Art. 15(2) of the NIS Directive (which lets authorities examine not only the results of an IT security audit but also the underlying findings) appear in section 8a, paragraphs (3) and (4).[85] Section 8b, paragraph 4 was amended to reflect that the verbal standard for mandatory reporting—a

---

[80] *Id.*
[81] *Id.*
[82] *Id.* at 36.
[83] *Id.*
[84] *Id.* at 39-40.
[85] *Id.* at 43.

"serious" incident—was to be applied in light of how seriously the event impacted the functionality of critical infrastructure. The seriousness of the event solely from the perspective of IT security would not be the basis for determining mandatory reporting.[86]

The BSI has made various materials available in English on its website.[87] More extensive materials are available in German.[88] The BSI publishes an extensive annual public service report on the status of IT security in Germany.[89]

VI.   AGENCY REGULATIONS

The 2017 amendments to the BSIG of 2009 were published along with agency regulations promulgated by the BMI pursuant to section 10 paragraph 1 of the BSIG in consultation with numerous other agencies of the German federal government.[90] Prior to amendment, regulations already existed specifying what would count as a "facility,"

---

[86] *Id.* at 47.

[87] *The BSI*, BUNDESAMT FÜR SICHERHEIT IN DER INFORMATIONSTECHNIK, https://www.bsi.bund.de/EN/TheBSI/thebsi_node.html (last visited December 20, 2017).

[88] *IT-Grundschutz*, BUNDESAMT FÜR SICHERHEIT IN DER INFORMATIONSTECHNIK, https://www.bsi.bund.de/DE/Themen/ITGrundschutz/itgrundschutz_no de.html (last visited December 20, 2017).

[89] The 2017 report can be accessed at *BSI-Lagebericht IT-Sicherheit*, BUNDESAMT FÜR SICHERHEIT IN DER INFORMATIONSTECHNIK, https://www.bsi.bund.de/DE/Publikationen/Lageberichte/lageberichte_ node.html (last visited Dec. 20, 2017).

[90] Erste Verordnung zur Änderung der BSI-Kritisverordnung vom 21. Juni 2017 [First regulation to modify the BSI *Kritis*-Regulation], June 29, 2017, BGBL I, 40, at 1903-1922, *available at* BUNDESANZEIGER VERLAG, http://mobile.bgbl.de/ (Ger.).

an "operator" and a "critical service" and quantifying a "degree of service" (Ger. *Versorgungsgrad*) and various threshold values that would determine whether the BSIG applied to a given operation.[91] These were actually the second of two rounds of updates begun under the previous IT Security Act. The first round dealt with the sectors energy, water and sewer, food, and IT and telecom.[92] The second round applied to the sectors healthcare,[93] insurance and financial services[94] and shipping and transportation.[95] Adjustments to prior regulations on water and sewer services were included with the second round.[96] Generally the threshold values are quantities such as, for example, gigawatt hours per year for an electrical transmission grid, or billions of liters of output per year for potable water.[97]

VII.   CYBERSECURITY AND THE NEW FEDERAL DATA PROTECTION ACT

In 2017, the Bundestag passed an act to repeal the Federal Data Protection Act of 2003[98] and implement the

---

[91] BSI-Kritisverordnung vom 22. April 2016 [BSI-KritisV] [Regulation on determining critical infrastructures under the BSIG], May 2, 2016, BGBL I, 20, at 958-969, as amended (Ger.), *available at* https://www.gesetze-im-internet.de/bsi-kritisv/index.html, § 1.

[92] *See id.*

[93] *Id.* § 6.

[94] *Id.* § 7.

[95] *Id.* § 8.

[96] *Id.* § 3.

[97] *See id.* (generally, various categories of annexes by sector with computation methods and formulas).

[98] Bundesdatenschutzgesetz in der Fassung der Bekanntmachung vom 14. Januar 2003 [Federal Data Protection Act in the version promulgated on January 14, 2003], January 14, 2003, BGBL I, 3, at 66-88, as amended. An officially commissioned English translation of the

GDPR.[99] The new Federal Data Protection Act (the "BDSG") implements the directly binding[100] GDPR along with provisions of national law which are permitted under various savings clauses in the GDPR. It will take effect on May 25, 2018. As of this writing an English translation of the new BDSG is available on the website of the International Association of Privacy Professionals.[101]

A provision of the former Act implicates IT security law, and the provision is substantially intact in the new Act. Section 9 of the old BDSG provides:

<u>Technical and organization measures</u>

Public and private bodies processing personal data either on their own behalf or on behalf of others shall take the technical and organizational measures necessary to ensure the implementation of the provisions of this Act, in particular the requirements set out in the annex to this Act. Measures shall be required only if the effort

---

Act, reflecting amendments through 2009, can be accessed for the time being at www.gesetze-im-internet.de/englisch_bdsg/englisch_bdsg.html (last accessed Dec. 17, 2017).

[99] Gesetz zur Anpassung des Datenschutzrechts an die Verordnung (EU) 2016/679 und zur Umsetzung der Richtlinie (EU) 2016/680 vom 30. Juni 2017 [DSAnpUG-EU] [An act to adapt data protection law to the Regulation (EU) 2016/679 and to give effect to the Directive (EU) 2016/680), June 30, 2017, BGBL I, 44, 2097-2132 [hereinafter the new BDSG], Art. 8(1), second sentence.

[100] EUROPEAN UNION, *supra* note 71.

[101] *The German Act to Adapt Data Protection Law to Regulation (EU) 2016/679 and to Implement Directive (EU) 2016/680 (English)*, IAPP, https://iapp.org/resources/article/the-german-act-to-adapt-data-protection-law-to-regulation-eu-2016679-and-to-implement-directive-eu-2016680-english/# (last visited December 17, 2017).

involved is reasonable in relation to the desired level of protection.[102]

The Annex specifies that "[w]here personal data are processed or used automatically, the internal organization of authorities or enterprises is to be arranged in such a way that it meets the specific requirement of data protection."[103]

The referenced Annex to the former BDSG specified the ends to be achieved by organizational means. Thus, no particular measures were required, but whatever was done had to be "suited to the type of personal data or data categories to be protected."[104] Access and use of data processing systems by unauthorized persons was to be prevented.[105] Authorized persons should have no access to data beyond their specific authorization. Personal data should not be available for unauthorized reading, copying, modification or removal during processing, storage, transport or transmission.[106] The destination of any personal data transmission had to be ascertainable, as did the identity of any persons inputting, modifying or removing data. Data processing agents were required to follow the principal's instructions strictly.[107] Personal data had to be protected from accidental destruction or loss, with data collected for different purposes being capable of separate processing.[108] The Annex expressly encouraged the use of encryption.[109]

---

[102] Federal Data Protection Act in the version promulgated on January 14, 2003, *supra* note 98, § 9, at 74.

[103] Federal Data Protection Act in the version promulgated on January 14, 2003, *supra* note 98, annex to § 9, at 88, first sentence.

[104] *Id.* second sentence.

[105] *Id.* second sentence nos. 1, 2.

[106] *Id.* second sentence no. 3.

[107] *Id.* second sentence nos. 4 – 6.

[108] *Id.* second sentence nos. 7 – 8.

[109] *Id.* third sentence.

Compare Art. 32(1) GDPR (security of processing) to this provision, which calls for

> [t]aking into account the state of the art, the costs of implementation and the nature, scope, context and purposes of processing as well as the risk . . . the [data] controller and the processor shall implement appropriate technical and organisational measures to ensure a level of security appropriate to the risk . . . .[110]

Letters (a) – (d) itemize "pseudonymisation" and encryption, ensuring confidentiality, integrity and authenticity ("CIA") plus resilience, timely recovery of systems after a physical or technical incident, and a process for regularly testing, assessing and evaluating the effectiveness of technical measures.[111]

The legal standards for IT security of critical infrastructure under the NIS Directive and BSIG closely resemble those for security of data processing under the GDPR and new BDSG. In particular, though data protection and IT security of critical infrastructure are formally distinct subject matter, the respective standards both refer to the state of the art and require measures proportionate to the associated risk of a breach.[112] Section 8a paragraph 1 of the

---

[110] Regulation (EU) 2016/679 of the European Parliament and of the Council of 27 April 2016 on the protection of natural persons with regard to the processing of personal data and on the free movement of such data, and repealing Directive 95/46/EC (General Data Protection Regulation), 2016 O.J. (L 119) 59, 1-30, http://eur-lex.europa.eu/eli/reg/2016/679/oj.

[111] *Id.* The rest of Art. 32, *i.e.*, paras. (2) – (4), refers to risk assessment, approval of codes of conduct and a certification mechanism, and control of natural persons acting under the authority of a data controller or processor.

[112] The corresponding provision of the new BDSG is at section 64

BSIG prescribes appropriate measures "not out of proportion to the consequences of a failure or disruption of an affected critical infrastructure." By comparison, appropriate measures are to be determined under section 64(1) of the new BDSG considering the state of the art, the cost of implementation, the type, extent, circumstances and purposes of data processing as well as the likelihood of incidence of a danger to the protected interests of the affected persons. The same norm calls for observance of the technical guidelines and recommendations of the BSI. Thus, when it comes to IT security in Germany and Europe, personal data is entitled to essentially the same level of protection as the potable water supply.

VIII.   PROPOSED   EU   REGULATION   OF   CYBERSECURITY PRODUCT CERTIFICATION IN THE COMMON MARKET AND ENISA AS THE EUROPEAN CYBERSECURITY AGENCY

This country brief concludes by drawing attention to the recently published European Commission proposed regulation of cybersecurity products. One of the stated aims of the proposed regulation is to get ahead of the plethora of ICT (that's information and communications technology) devices on the horizon to achieve a high level of cybersecurity.[113] The proposal foresees making ENISA—

Anforderungen an die Sicherheit der Datenverarbeitung [Requirements for the security of data processing]. *See* the new BDSG, *supra* notes 99 (Ger.) & 101; *see also* SCHAFFLAND/WILTFANG, DS-GVO Art. 32 *Vorbemerkung* [preliminary remark] & paras. 4, 5, 140, *available at* WWW.DATENSCHUTZDIGITAL.DE by subscription (Ger.).

[113] *Commission Proposal*, *supra* note 9 (citing for instance connected and automated cars, electronic health systems and industrial automation control systems, or "IACS"). The proposed text of the regulation begins at p. 22.

the European Union's cybersecurity agency located in Greece—into a permanent agency with an expanded mandate. One mandate would be to establish sector-specific information sharing hubs called "Information Sharing and Analysis Centres."[114] ENISA would also oversee market-related tasks such as standardization and certification of products.[115] The aim is to avoid internal fragmentation of the single European market for cybersecurity product certification.[116] The proposed regulation and public comments are found on the website of the European Commission.[117] Around the same time the European Commission published this proposal, it also issued a recommendation on coordinated response to large-scale cybersecurity incidents and crises.[118]

---

[114] *Id.* at 4-7.

[115] *Id.* at 7.

[116] *See id.* at 9-10 & n.15.

[117] *See* Cybersecurity Package, EUROPEAN COMMISSION, https://ec.europa.eu/info/law/better-regulation/initiatives/com-2017-477_en (last visited Dec. 20, 2017).

[118] Commission Recommendation (EU) 2017/1584 of 13 September 2017 on Coordinated Response to Large-Scale Cybersecurity Incidents and Crises, C/2017/6100, O.J. (L 239) 60, 36 – 58, http://eur-lex.europa.eu/legal-content/EN/TXT/PDF/?uri=CELEX:32017H1584&from=EN.

About the Journal of Law and Cyber Warfare
The Journal of Law and Cyber Warfare is published twice per
year by top legal professionals and scholars from the law,
technology, security, and business industries. The views
expressed in the Journal of Law and Cyber Warfare are those of
the authors and not necessarily of the Journal of Law and Cyber
Warfare or Lexeprint Inc. — the publishing company.

Submissions
The Journal welcomes submissions from legal scholars,
technologists, mathematicians, analysts, academics, policy
makers, practitioners, lawyers, judges and social scientists.

Form: Citations conform to The Bluebook: A Uniform System
of Citation (20th ed. 2015). Please cite the Journal of Law and
Cyber Warfare as: 6 J.L. & CYBER WARFARE ___ (2018).

Copyright: All articles copyright © 2012-2018 by the Journal of
Law and Cyber Warfare except where otherwise expressly
indicated. For all articles to which it holds copyright, the Journal
of Law and Cyber Warfare permits copies to be made for
classroom use, provided that (1) the author and the Journal of
Law and Cyber Warfare are identified, (2) the proper notice of
copyright is affixed to each copy, (3) each copy is distributed at
or below cost, and (4) the Journal of Law and Cyber Warfare is
notified of the use.

Electronic submissions are encouraged. Submissions by email
and attachment should be directed to submissions@jlcw.org.

Subscriptions: The cost of an annual subscription is $250.
Subscription requests should be e-mailed to info@jlcw.org.

Internet Address: The Journal of Law and Cyber Warfare
website is located at www.jlcw.org.